Film and Censorship

Over the past quarter of a century, *Index on Censorship* has been an unflinching witness to the many and varied workings of tyranny, from the persecution of dissidents behind the Iron Curtain to Latin America's 'dirty wars' and the troubled legacy of colonialism in Africa. By the same token, the magazine has also borne eloquent testimony to the flipside of repression, to the human spirit's extraordinary capacity for survival and its unquenchable appetite for freedom. In the process, *Index* has published some of the world's finest writers, sharpest analysts and foremost thinkers all of whom, at one time or another, have been exercised by questions of rights, liberties, toleration and dissent. This series brings together some of the most important materials from twenty-five years of *Index* according to theme, beginning with *The Fall of Communism and the Rise of Nationalism* and *Film and Censorship*.

Lancaster House
33 Islington High Street
London N1 9LH
Telephone: (0171) 278 2313
Fax: (0171) 278 1878
e-mail: indexcenso@gn.apc.org

Film and Censorship

The **INDEX** Reader

Edited by Ruth Petrie
Introduced by Sheila Whitaker

CASSELL
London and Washington

Cassell
Wellington House
125 Strand
London WC2R 0BB

PO Box 605
Herndon
Virginia 20172

First published 1997

British Library Cataloguing-in-Publication Data
A catalogue record for this book is available from the British Library.

Library of Congress Cataloging-in-Publication Data
Film and censorship : the Index reader / edited by Ruth Petrie; introduced by Sheila Whitaker.
    p. cm.
    Includes index.
    ISBN 0-304-33936-9 (hc). – ISBN 0-304-33937-7 (pbk.)
    1. Motion pictures—Censorship. I. Petrie, Ruth. II. Index on censorship.
PN1995.6.F56   1997
363.3′ 1—dc21
                                                                97-160
                                                                CIP

ISBN 0–304–33936–9 (hardback)
     0–304–33937–7 (paperback)

Cover still: Malcolm McDowell in Stanley Kubrick's *A Clockwork Orange*. BFI Stills, Posters and Designs, courtesy of the Roland Grant Archive.

Typeset by BookEns Ltd, Royston, Herts.
Printed and bound in Great Britain by Biddles Ltd, Guildford and King's Lynn

Contents

CONTENTS

Editorial note

The essays in this collection have been reprinted from *Index on Censorship* in their original form apart from minor alterations. No attempt has been made to update political, social and artistic references.

Acknowledgement

Grateful acknowledgement is made to the individuals who have given permission for their articles to be included in this collection.

Introduction

Sheila Whitaker

It is not only appropriate but timely that the twenty-fifth anniversary celebrations of *Index on Censorship* should include this collection of essays on film. Appropriate and timely inasmuch as, with its first century behind it, film (in all its forms) has increasingly been perceived as having a harmful influence on society. Film has aroused protests of horror from its earliest days, but the protestations have, over the century, become ever more vociferous, pervasive, and more dangerously, are now transformed into action.

As these essays make clear, the manifestations of censorship have taken a variety of forms throughout the world. Foremost, of course, is the act of censorship in its clearest and most unambiguous form – the refusal of the relevant authorities to allow a film or films to be seen. This happens throughout the world, including in the West. However, as we all know, other forms of censorship are not always as obvious as outright banning and therefore are harder to resist or protest. These more discreet censorings can take the form of prior censorship, such as the refusal by dictatorships to permit a film to be made or, as happens in Western 'democratic' societies, the refusal of funding, particularly from government sources such as the National Endowment for the Arts Fund in the USA which, during the Bush years, became almost entirely subject to the Republicans' right-wing agenda. It can also manifest itself in post-censorship, whether it be the re-editing and/or cutting of a film's original version (see James Ivory on *The Wild Party* ('Hollywood versus Hollywood') p. 5 and Frank Rich on Ophuls' *The Memory of Justice* ('Justice for Ophuls?' p. 17).

It is, of course, easy for 'democratic' societies to take a 'holier than thou' approach to the subject when they can point their fingers at state censorship as practised in China and the former Soviet Union and even easier when dictatorships (military or otherwise) arrest or murder film-makers. A.J. Liehm's article on Czechoslovak cinema ('Thaws, Booms and Blacklists' p. 71) during the 1960s vividly reminded me of my visit to Prague in 1986 to research a major historical retrospective on Czechoslovakian cinema. The national archive was opened to me – except where 1960s film was concerned. This was not entirely surprising. Indeed the individuals with whom I was dealing were open about the problems (there was no bureaucratic obfuscation) and disappointed at the ban. All they could do was shrug their shoulders and recognize that we were most likely to show the films which had made it to the West. Those that were banned have still to be seen. We in the West could have felt smug about this, but is our record that much better? It is not. Where dictatorships – lacking any pretensions to democracy – have largely pursued their acts of aggression against film-makers, Western governments – as alert to the apparent dangers of film as any dictatorship but having to accede to the pretence if not the essence of democratic institutions – tend to focus more on the audience and the need for its protection. (The major, infamous exception to this is of course the McCarthy hearings of the 1950s.) As Guy Phelps points out,

> [In 1909] the cinema had been blamed for almost every social calamity of the preceding decade with the possible exception of the Boer War. Clergymen, police chiefs and right-thinking people everywhere inveighed against this venal form of entertainment which was available to the poor and illiterate

Philip French also reminds us that, for example, *Battleship Potemkin* was refused a certificate in Britain for 30 years, and in 1958 Stanley Kubrick's *Paths of Glory* was banned in France. Until the mid-sixties theatre productions in Britain were subject to the edict of the Lord Chamberlain. It was only in 1960 that D. H. Lawrence's novel *Lady Chatterley's Lover* was unsuccessfully prosecuted for obscenity. Today – particularly in the UK and the USA – the dimensions of the problem are even greater as the media take up (perhaps more often make up) and run with wildly exaggerated stories of the impact of films, leading to suggestions of, for example, 'copycat' killings, all of this coinciding with the proliferation of new technologies. Governments verge on panic if they foresee political disadvantage in not responding to the media's claim to be the voice of the 'moral majority'. Draconian video classification legislation vividly manifests the outcome of these coincidences in Britain.

To say all this is not to ignore the need for all societies in all periods of history to maintain cohesion, and a universal recognition of what is acceptable and what is not. Nor is it to ignore the fact that children need to be protected. The problem arises when those in power, alert to the need to protect and maintain state authority, refuse the basic right of all adults to create and, in the context of film, other adults to view what they wish: social cohesion, and all that flows from it, arises from a consensus within the population itself, not from an imposed ethic. I am aware that such a position may appear simplistic, not to say naïve, in the world of the late twentieth century, but this right is still unalienable. Democracy, at its best, will inevitably promote a healthy balance in society. Censorship, whether it be against the act of creation or the act of viewing, is unacceptable.

These essays are a powerful reminder of the ever-continuing acts against human rights that are perpetrated throughout the world, whether by dictatorships in the cause of state control, or by democracies in the name of our protection.

As part of the growing pre-election sex and violence hysteria in Britain (this is written in January 1997) we have most recently been subjected to a media witch-hunt of David Cronenberg's *Crash*. This came after Home Secretary Michael Howard took up a political position in favour of stricter censorship with Labour's Jack Cunningham following his lead in a cringing act of political cowardice and self-interest. Not to be outdone, Virginia Bottomley, Heritage Secretary capitalized on the media hysteria. She urged all local councils to ban the film. (Need I add that neither she nor any of the journalists who called for it to be banned had actually seen it.) In other words, as election battles commence, even the most cursory nod towards civil rights has been abandoned by media and politicians alike as they vie with each other for the (supposed) moral high ground. And the even more dangerous idea of the British Board of Film Classification becoming an arm of government hovers in the air.

These are dangerous times and we have to be ever more vigilant, active and vocal in defence of our rights: if we fail to make our voices heard we shall undoubtedly live to rue the day as the free circulation of ideas and basic civil rights disappears both at home and abroad.

Hollywood versus Hollywood

James Ivory

The term 'the final cut' in commercial film-making has an ominous sound to the layman, who cannot understand how it is possible for the director of a film to have his work re-edited by others against his wishes. The final cut and who has the right to make it is an issue that has been fought over by the creators of films and those who have the controlling financial interest in them since the beginning of the film industry. Unless his contract protects that right, so basic to any kind of personal expression in films, the director will usually lose this last battle, though he may have won all the others in the course of making his film. Once he has done everything else satisfactorily, his masters may now decide they can afford to dispense with his services. Since few directors in English-speaking countries are ever powerful enough to demand and get the final cut, history provides many examples of mutilated works, major and minor.

When a director has been ousted from his editing room, all appeals to reason having failed, he may find allies among the powerful stars who have acted in his film. Or he can go to influential critics, who may be willing to take up his cause in the newspapers. But once the altered version of his film is before the public, there is little chance that it will be recalled in favour of the one acceptable to him, and it will continue to play, for better or worse, usually giving everyone a bad name: director, writer, actors, and – finally – the persons responsible for the mutilation.

This form of censorship, undertaken for commercial reasons, is in some ways as effective as any applied by totalitarian regimes to suppress dissent. And the men who carry out this work so eagerly are often, psychologically, like the petty functionaries the state employs for its purposes: former advertising executives, accountants, lawyers, agents turned showmen – frustrated 'artists' who are thereby given a chance to meddle with the work of genuine artists. These latter, however, they often fear and hate, and treat with contempt – despite the show of deference due to the supposedly exalted position of film directors. Let a film be reviewed badly or, much worse, be a flop, and you will see that deference transformed into a gross contempt expressed, in some cases, by the physical destruction of the film itself. In the atmosphere of panic which is created whenever the investment in a picture seems threatened by early bad (or sometimes merely contradictory) reaction to it, fumbling attempts to make it 'work' are hastily made by the studio functionaries – who also scramble to get out of the cursed shadow of the failure as fast as possible. But this rarely manages to save a film or make it more palatable in the public.

Some films fail because they are bad. The public sees this at once and stays away. Sometimes, however, the public is put off a good picture because of an accident in timing: the appearance of a favourite star in a guise which is unacceptable; a directorial style which is not accessible to a mass audience; a story which has a depressing effect on people. No re-editing has ever saved these kinds of failed film, good or bad, or turned them into box-office successes. Time alone works to redeem a distinguished failure, but too slowly to do anybody much immediate good, and certainly not fast enough to save the financier's investment.

Sometimes a case can be made for the studio presented with a finished film which really is too long, and might tax the patience of the public. One can certainly sympathize with the distributor without advocating hasty trimming. And many disciplined directors have coolly cut excess footage without regrets once they've seen how their film played. But this is a different situation from that of the filmmaker whose work is taken away from him and drastically altered: when the story line is changed so that the purpose and point of view of director and writer are made unclear; when material is removed that is needed to reveal the characters, while other material already discarded by the director is introduced to provoke easy laughs or prurient interest; in which the style and texture of the piece have been debased.

Such was the case with *The Wild Party*, which started out to be a Hollywood-in-the-Twenties musical, and which, in its patched-together remnants, proves once more that you cannot effectively re-edit a picture and change its character in order allegedly to 'save' it.

Selling nostalgia
American International must have thought that if they backed a film called *The Wild Party* starring Raquel Welch, and let it be identified

with the squalid Fatty Arbuckle scandal ('A Night of Gin and Sin, a Night They're Still Whispering About'!), they wouldn't have to do anything else: they could sit back and let the money pour in from small town drive-ins, as well as cash in on the current craze for nostalgia in somewhat more sophisticated places. They thought the film was nostalgic because it was set in 1929 and the extras wore a lot of beaded dresses and wing-tip collars and talked about the swell party over at Doug and Mary's. But did they *look* at that collection of bleary-eyed drunks carousing in a dishevelled mansion and think they were selling nostalgia? Did they look at anything? When press agents dictated blurbs about Hollywood decadence, did anyone stop to ask: what decadence? In 1929, Hollywood was entering its Golden Age, and its citizens, who are presented in the film, were taking part in a gold rush, like pioneers. They were not decadents, but on the contrary, rather wholesome people, getting rich and having fun, as they invented both an art form and an entertainment industry. That is what the film is about; the story tells of a silent-screen actor's professional downfall and personal collapse. It was meant to be taken seriously – but not so seriously that there was no room for the songs and dances which are an outgrowth of the party's natural action and which were intended to lighten the mood. These carefully choreographed numbers were also casualties in the massive re-editing. How did all this happen? How does a film, carrying its loads of hope and gold, sink as easily as this one did?

The Wild Party is based on a blank verse narrative poem written by Joseph Moncure March in 1926. The action originally took place in Greenwich Village at a party thrown by a vaudeville comic in his walk-up apartment. When it was published it had a kind of underground success due to its frankness, but today the poem's charm lies in its jazzy rhythms and period slang. To try to make a film with American International out of such material would perhaps seem to many readers an act of madness. To accept money (but who refuses an offer of money to make a film?) from such a source might seem to be either calculating or an act of extreme innocence. But then, encountering the poetry in the script (the setting had been shifted to California, though the characters, in their Hollywood equivalents, were the same), which was sometimes to be spoken directly to the camera by the poet-narrator, and many other 'artsy-fartsy' touches as Sam Arkoff, the owner of American International put it, why go ahead and back the film at all, especially when it was to be directed by 'that mystic' – myself? Arkoff is supposed to have said that he took up this dubious project because of its enticing sounding title, and because of the presence of Raquel Welch as Queenie, though he is also supposed to have said that the mystic would turn her into Doris Day. Yet one can plainly see that it was a fine and daring thing of American International to go into such a venture. Arkoff alludes to his involvement with some pride in a story about him printed in the *New York Times*. So what went wrong?

The not so final cut

When the first rough-cut of the film was shown to American International, few misgivings were expressed about the picture as a whole. The film was too long, running two hours and a quarter and the pacing was erratic, but the mood at AIP's offices on Wiltshire Boulevard was one of cautious optimism. After this first screening there was a 'creative' session. We went down a list prepared during the screening by Arkoff's associates, who had huddled together in the dark scribbling comments down on a clipboard to which a little light had been attached. This light kept going on and off, signalling displeasure I felt sure, yet some of their suggestions were excellent. Others were merely frivolous, an annoyance, and the rest were bad. We went back to New York, where the film was being edited, determined to carry out the good suggestions, to ignore the others, and generally to do the things to it which we felt were necessary.

After a month, when the length of the film had been reduced to a little under two hours, we were again summoned to the Coast for another screening and another creative encounter session in AIP's boardroom. Now the mood had changed. Sam Arkoff was 'disappointed'. The film didn't *move*. There were further suggestions, each person putting forth his ideas about this or that scene. Edgar Lansbury, one of the executive producers, was also there, looking grave. Probably he had been taken aside and made to listen to doubts about my editing methods, which seemed not to be getting us anywhere. But as he had supported me through the turbulent shooting, I was confident I would retain control of the film's final form. We returned to New York and another list appeared a few days later. There were new suggestions on it, as well as all the old ones we hadn't taken seriously. Although this kind of interference is forbidden by an agreement the major movie-making companies have with the Directors' Guild of America, to which I belong, I removed another ten minutes from the film. I was not unhappy to lose ten minutes; but American International was by now telling me *which* minutes, for example insisting that I shorten Raquel Welch's big number, *Singapore Sally*, and sending me detailed instructions to show me how they would do it if they were editing the film. Their demands were challenges. Not to combat, but to find satisfactory solutions.

When the film's running time was down to an hour and 48 minutes I decided that was as much as I could do to oblige American International. It was not only a matter of what was right for the film; their harrying us all the time was going to put us off schedule. The editor, Kent McKinney, was afraid we would never be ready with our sound tracks by the time of the re-recording, a date set months before. Arkoff sent two of his creative consultants on a quick trip to New York to see my 'final cut' before the re-recording started. They didn't like the film at all. But Lansbury and his partner, Joseph Beruh, were getting fed up with all this meddling and they sent the Vice-Presidents back to the West Coast unsatisfied. The film was mixed, the negative was cut, and the first prints were ordered. I felt the picture was substantially as I had wanted it. The battles of shooting, the sessions with AIP in Beverly Hills – all that was forgotten in the feeling of euphoria (short-lived, in this case) everyone shares when a film is completed and, one believes, completed well. Yet my presence at, or around, the delivered film was resented. When I went to Hollywood to be on hand while the prints were being 'timed' at Movielab in the absence of the cameraman, Walter Lassally, who was in England, I was made to feel I was being humoured in some last act of self-indulgence. I knew what effects Lassally wanted – how light, how dark, etc. – and the grading man was wonderfully cooperative, but it was sometimes hard to get my recommendations carried out. American International's head of post-production always sat in the theatre. I would have to hear things like: 'You have these fantastic sets, what do you want to make them so dark for?' They were afraid that, after more than a year on the project, after having brought it through several script re-writes, the casting, very difficult shooting, and the editing, the director would not somehow wreck everything. It was time, they felt, for the *real* professionals to take over.

Ismail Merchant, the producer, now wanted to show his new film to a few friends and to persons who could be trusted to write usefully about it. He wanted to be able to start promoting it, in his usual energetic way. But American International was afraid that he, too, would spoil everything. It seemed obvious to him to open the film in New York and Los Angeles in prestige theatres as quickly as possible, while there were the benefits of the considerable advance publicity to help the film, and before the other Hollywood period piece, *Day of the Locust*, made its appearance. But this would have been a radical departure from AIP's regular and highly successful grab-a-buck-and-run distribution pattern: saturation booking away from the media centres and then, when the picture is in profit and it no longer matters whether the critics pan it or not, bringing it to the major cities. With the greatest misgivings, AIP turned over one of its prints to the producer and to Edgar Lansbury, who also wanted to elicit some opinions, and this was taken to New York. Simultaneously, they began to speak of a shorter version of the film, one playing for 95 or a hundred minutes. But we felt that if we could get a few powerful New York critics to come out for the film, AIP might be discouraged from tampering with it. However, our strongest ally was to be Raquel Welch herself, who was now shown the finished film. She was excited by it and by the response of critics like Arthur Knight and Judith Crist, who had seen the picture and found her performance a revelation of unsuspected – or at least up to then unrealized – talents for acting comedy and for singing and dancing. We held a general screening in New York for a hundred guests and followed that with a big party. Our reading of the audience reaction was that people had liked the film very much and this was backed up by the comments of the critics. We felt the chances for the film were good, given the right send-off.

In the same week (that of January 27–February 2 1975), AIP held two 'sneak' previews of the film, one in Santa Barbara, the other in San Diego. There are no attempts at advance secrecy any more when sneaks are held; ads are put in the local papers giving the name of the new film, which plays for a night on a double bill with the picture already running in the theatre. Cards are passed out to the audience to fill up. The questions asked of the audiences for *The Wild Party* in the two cities were:

What scenes did you enjoy the most?
What scenes did you like the least, if any?
Would you recommend this film to your friends?
If so, what particular scene would you relate in recommending it?
How would you rate this film? (Excellent, good, fair, poor)

Sex and age were asked, and there was space on the card for additional comments. Both previews turned out disastrously. The atmosphere in the theatre at Santa Barbara had been particularly frightening. The reaction to *The Wild Party* had been one of loathing. The audience was composed mainly of students from the adjoining University of California campus and they jeered at the film. Their most violent reactions seemed, judging from the cards they filled out, to be against Raquel Welch and the young leading man, Perry King. They wanted the old, slam-bang, camp Raquel, not the new, serious, vulnerable one we gave them, and they hated Perry King's sleek looks and immaculate evening dress and immaculate accent. The only things the students liked were the 'orgy' scene – a kind of erotic musical number which was cut in Great Britain – and a fight. But in San Diego everything was reversed. *Singapore Sally*, at which the students had hooted, was the high point for this predominantly middle-class audience, and Raquel, who grew up in San Diego, was much praised in the cards. Not much else was. The 'orgy' and the violence were disliked, and there were many walk-outs, each one noted by an announcement made into a tape recorder brought to the theatre by an AIP executive. Joe Beruh had gone to California to be present at the two previews and to report back on what happened and on what AIP would do next. Both partners had a lot of money tied up in the film; it was important to get it in front of the public right away. But now, understandably, AIP was in no hurry to open the picture. The two previews had upset everything and were causing further confusion by being contradictory.

Joe Beruh returned to New York with a message from Sam Arkoff: Did Ivory have any ideas how the film might be shortened?

I was glad to be asked my opinion at this late stage, but I felt I needed to look at the film with a different editor and I engaged Alan Heim, fresh from *Lenny*, to help me trim it. We worked for two days and managed to remove eight more minutes – but Heim did this so cleverly that it was very hard to tell anything had been done. From AIP's point of view this wasn't much help. It was the same film, minus some entrances and exits and bits of dialogue. No editorial magic had turned it into the film of their dreams. Meanwhile, without telling me, Lansbury and Beruh made up their own list of proposed cuts and sent it out to California. They were getting itchy; they wanted – who didn't? – to get on to other things. We urged the distributor to release the film in New York before any more time passed. We were confident that it would find a following and that the New York press would support us, despite the debacle of the two previews. We pointed to all the hits that had been booed during their sneak previews. We were getting rather desperate. AIP was now talking about making Jolly Grimm, the main character of the film (played by James Coco), into a more lovable man. Audiences could not identify with someone so choleric they said. We begged for the film to be given a chance as made, but this only made them angry. Who were we to tell them how to market the picture? We withdrew at this point and I began to edit my next film, *Autobiography of a Princess*.

Raquel Welch now heard that the film was being totally re-cut in Hollywood by AIP's own editor. She instructed her lawyers to notify the distributor that she would do no publicity for the picture until she saw for herself how this new version turned out. They tried to reassure her: they told her she would love the new, exciting, Felliniesque version of *The Wild Party*. But when she saw it, she hated what they'd done to the picture and threatened to sue if they put it into release. More time passed, during which Lansbury and Beruh, followed by Walter Marks, who wrote the screenplay and much of the music, saw and approved the re-edited version, which ran ninety minutes – Sam Arkoff's magic number. People began to ask: Whatever happened to *The Wild Party*? It was going around that there was some problem with the picture. And when film festivals tried to show it, AIP refused permission.

Disastrous reviews

In late spring 1975 there seemed to be a change of heart. Whether due to the pressure kept up on them by Raquel, or a negative reaction from exhibitors to the re-edited version of the film, American International decided to release my cut everywhere – that is, in the hundred-minute form Alan Heim and I had prepared. There had been talk of showing two versions, mine in the cities, theirs in small towns; preparations were now made to a kind of selected city approach. We were ecstatic, and threw a big party in New York so that the press could meet the stars of the film. But the question everybody asked was: When is the picture having its New York premiere? It had opened in Washington and was due to play in Boston and Denver; what about New York? During the party, a well-wisher sent us an envelope containing the first reviews, from Washington. They were terrible. We did not show them to Raquel, but their import was ominous: she had gone to Washington to promote the film and the same papers that had carried her interviews and photographs now ridiculed her performance. And business was terrible, too. The same thing was repeated in Boston. Savage reviews, bad box-office. After this, the film was withdrawn from release.

It was now summer; six months had passed since the film had been delivered to the distributor. It existed in a limbo of rumour. No one could find out anything definite; the anxious co-stars were fobbed off with stories of an imminent opening which kept being put further and further ahead: 16 June, 26 June, then 26 July, etc. I was told nothing at all. But our fears that the re-edited version of the film would now be generally released – the Ivory version having been 'market-tested' and found unsaleable – seemed confirmed by an event which seems like one of Fate's grand coincidences. Ismail Merchant, in London in connection with *Autobiography of a Princess*, heard, as he was screening that film for some friends, the music of *The Wild Party* coming through the wall of an adjoining screening room on Wardour Street. He went into the projection booth to watch and to ask who was being shown the film. A delegation of Rank exhibitors was seeing the AIP cut of the picture before its release in England. When told of this I wrote to Sam Arkoff, threatening to take the whole thing up in the newspapers, but this letter was ignored, as all our others had been.

The English release of the picture was being handled by a company called Seven Keys, who showed it to the trade papers and monthly magazines in early August. This screening was presided over by Andrew Gatty, the head of Seven Keys, who spoke of bringing a new optimism to the British film industry; 'entertainment' was to be the key word. Later, when asked privately by our solicitor whether he knew of the existence of the director's version of the film, he said, oh, yes, he had preferred it to the one being released, but Rank had turned it down. He had asked Rank to have another look and had only reluctantly shown them the AIP version, which they took. What could he do? Artistically, Ivory's was the version he liked, but he was also a businessman: if he hadn't accepted Rank's offer, *The Wild Party* would never have been shown in England at all.

All I could now do was write to the British film critics to explain what had happened to *The Wild Party*. My letter appeared the day the film opened in London and brought the first communication I had had from AIP in months. It was a furious one, consisting of charges of having damaged the film's chances for a commercial success by defaming it in print, and of deliberately trying to sabotage those chances, for which I would be held personally responsible. This was soon followed by a letter from Seven Keys' General Manager, James Robinson, who was 'shocked and appalled' that I would take it upon myself to made such damaging comments about the film and, by inference, about Seven Keys, whose credibility as renters to the cinemas and as suppliers of the product to the public had been unfairly damaged by my irresponsible action. This, he said, had had the effect of associating his company with the 'cheap attempt to over-exploit everything exploitable' with which my letter had charged AIP's editors. He wrote:

> We have spent a great deal of time, a great deal of money and a great deal of thought in the promotion of this picture not at all with a view to simple exploitation, but within the serious philosophy of our company of making sure that all our advertising and promotion work attracts the sort of person who, when he sees the film, will be in no way disappointed. We take great pains *not* to mislead ...

Seven Keys required my assurance that I would 'immediately desist' from writing all these bad things. They too were going to hold me responsible for the 'devastating effect' my letter had on business. One could not help asking at this point why, if Seven Keys had spent all that time, money, and thought on the film's promotion, they had opened it on a double bill with an old Mel Brooks film, and at the Astoria, which John Coleman, in his sympathetic review in the *New Statesman* called 'that great graveyard on Charing Cross Road where celluloid white elephants go to die'. Or why they had not bothered to invite the critics of the daily and Sunday London papers to a press show, but had caused them to go out and buy tickets in order to see the film. But all this hullabaloo seems not to have had that adverse effect on the picture's chances after all, rather the contrary, and it had a perfectly decent run of several weeks. *Variety* reported business as being good.

Since then, the film has played here and there around the United States in the AIP version and on Home Box Office – subscription television. It has still to open in New York and so, *officially*, has not opened at all. It is becoming legendary, one likes to think. As it recedes in time from the days of expectation when it was being made, hopes for it fade for everybody who took part in it. For Raquel Welch, who, after her success in *The Three Musketeers*, wanted to do something challenging and unlike anything she had ever done before; for Jimmy Coco, who needed a grand, starring vehicle to show off *his* talents; for Merchant Ivory Productions, who hoped against hope for an American-style commercial success; for Lansbury and Beruh, who wanted to make some money while enlarging the scope of their showmanship; for Walter Marks, whose dream *The Wild Party* was, and who, in his innocence, tried to make an expressionistic screen musical with sex, murder, and poetry; and finally for American International Pictures, who, despite all talk to the contrary, wanted 'to go straight' and to do something they could be proud of.

Recut films: some examples

There are hundreds of films which have been re-edited against the wishes of their directors, including many considered to be classics. A short list of recut films would include: Abel Gance's *Napoléon*, so dangerously innovative at the time (1927) that Metro Goldwyn Mayer bought it supposedly to ensure that the film would never be seen by the public as made; Von Stroheim's ten-hour *Greed*; Murnau's *City Girl*, retitled *Our Daily Bread*; Vigo's *L'Atalante*. Closer to our times there have been films like Vidor's *Northwest Passage*; Welles' *The Magnificent Ambersons*; Huston's *The Red Badge of Courage*; Cukor's

A Star Is Born; Max Ophul's *Lola Montez*; Ford's *Seven Women*. Most recently there have been a number of Peckinpah films – *Pat Garrett and Billy the Kid*; *Major Dundee*; *The Get-Away* (its star, Steve McQueen, had the final cut); Altman's *Brewster McCloud*; Polansky's *The Fearless Vampire Killers*; Reisz's *The Loves of Isadora*. (Reisz's years of experience as a top feature editor could not save his film from being recut by Universal Pictures, and it is not reported that that studio's editors followed Reisz's textbook on editing techniques when they recut the picture.) American International Pictures has also had a history of practising reverse alchemy, of trying to turn gold into dross. They like to point out today that they gave Francis Coppola and Martin Scorsese their first big break, but they recut the former's *Dementia 13* and the latter's *Boxcard Bertha*. Both directors have disowned these films.

Justice for Ophuls?

Frank Rich

During the first week of this month, as we woke up to discover that America's Dien Bien Phu was at hand in Vietnam, I spent the better part of a day in an airless room in New York City watching a film that at once sums up this searing historical moment and looks beyond it – a film that bridges the gap between the inevitable conclusion of any ugly war and the next chapter ahead, that postwar epilogue that is finally ours to make of what we will. The film is called *The Memory of Justice*, and it is the latest documentary by Marcel Ophuls, the filmmaker whose 1971 documentary about Vichy France, *The Sorrow and the Pity*, is a classic against which all nonfiction cinema must be measured. Like *Sorrow*, *Memory* is a four-and-half-hour long exploration of the legacy of World War II, but it has its own special focus. Ophuls' new film is about the war crimes trials at Nuremburg, about how the justice dispensed there holds up against the test of time and how the legal and moral principles established then might be of value to us now. Ophuls doesn't have glib answers to these questions – his movie is rich in contradictions, difficult nuances, anguish and doubt – and he constructs his argument with a scrupulous and painstaking respect for all permutations of the truth. By the time the film was over, I was bleary-eyed with exhaustion, but also peculiarly high – as if suddenly past, present and future had become a continuum, as if I had learned for the first time how to swim with the currents of history, how to see events extending beyond my years clearly and see them whole.

Unfortunately, my pleasure in recounting the experience of seeing this remarkable film is tempered sorely by my knowledge that, as I sit here writing about it, the odds are that this movie will be lost forever to the public. After a series of conflicts of a kind that are endemic to relationships between showbiz hustlers and artists who have the gall to insist on creative autonomy, *Memory* has been taken out of Ophuls' hands by its London-based producers, David Puttnam and Sanford Lieberson, and turned over to a German director who is now recutting Ophuls' original, finished print. The break between the director and the money men came last December when Ophuls, long engaged in an acrimonious debate with Puttnam and Lieberson over the aesthetic, political and commercial worthiness of his film, stormed out of a meeting at the Ritz Hotel bar in London after the producers announced their intention to recut the film for the American market. The producers decided to interpret Ophuls' walkout as a decision to walk off the film entirely, and, since that time, the new version of *Memory* has been readied for submission to the BBC and the German co-producer, Polytel, who hold European options on the project, as well as for potential American distributors. While Ophuls may ultimately prove that the producers had created a pretext to get rid of him so that they could then recut the picture to their own tastes, his rights under British law are ambiguous enough to allow Puttnam and Lieberson to distribute their version of *Memory* while litigation unfolds. In the end, if Ophuls were to 'win' his case, the victory might be a Pyrrhic one – the recut movie would be in distribution (without a director's credit), his own cut would be doomed to oblivion, and he would gain only financial restitution.

The circumstances under which I and several other film critics saw Ophuls' version of the film in New York this month were extraordinary. A work print of his final cut of *Memory* had been brought into this country unbeknownst to either Ophuls or the picture's producers and was made available to us by an Ophuls rooter who wished to get the story of the director's plight out in the open. The picture was shown on an editing machine that projects the image on a screen about the size of a 15" television set. It was the worst possible conditions under which to watch a film, especially one of this length, and yet even without benefit of colour (which, for economy's sake, is duplicated in black-and-white in a work print), even with a manually improvised sound mix and 20-minute breaks in continuity as reels were changed, *Memory* is a riveting piece of work.

Triumph of the Untalented

A. J. Liehm

In the sixties Czechoslovak cinema was one of the most remarkable in the world. At a time when film making had become completely commercialized, it managed to devote as much as 30 per cent of its feature-film production to the output of artistically ambitious movies. At a time when, everywhere from Hollywood to Moscow, utter cynicism prevailed, with the result that the studios churned out artistically mediocre ideological stereotypes whose sole aim was to satisfy the producers and reassure them that everything was well in the best of all possible worlds – at this time the authors of Czech and Slovak films (many of them commercially viable) posed questions, to themselves and the world, irrespective of whether East, West, North or South, about the fundamental problems of man's humanity, about the relationship between the individual and society, about power and helplessness, sincerity and hypocrisy. They sought to discover the mainsprings of bourgeois attitudes, of brutality and oppression, refusing to resort to conventional lies as they attempted to bring to light the truth about the past, buried under mountains of empty rhetoric. They did not show the viewer characters manipulated by a police state, a cynical ideocracy or a consumer society, but rather they portrayed men and women as we know them, with all their virtues and failings, attractive as well as repulsive, truly alive as well as undergoing a living death, loving (unhappily) as well as hating (happily), treating their subject-matter with the fearless honesty of the true artist. And in order to do all this they had to invent their own idiom, pioneering rather than emulating, because for what they wanted to express there were no models, either for images, style or words. They took a fresh look at the world. And people all over the world admired them or booed them, as is the case with all true art. Only one thing they did not know, which was to come later – indifference. The indifference of audiences as well as film-makers.

In those years Czechoslovakia, a small country with an annual output of 35 full-length feature films, had some 25 film directors of international stature and repute. Not to mention the directors of shorts, documentaries, popular-scientific and animated films. And those who worked exclusively (or almost exclusively) for television and were again among the world's best in this new medium.

For the first time since the days of the Soviet avant garde, socialist cinematography showed that it does not have to deal in boundless mediocrity, in picturebook realism à la Hollywood decked out in socialist trappings, in dreary conformity, boredom, beer-hall or operetta humour, that it does not have to toady to the establishment by turning out holy pictures and sentimental *kitsch* full of a false, hypo-critical morality. It went on to demonstrate this, not for one year, two or three, as had the Poles and the Hungarians in the fifties or the Yugoslavs a decade later, but for some seven or eight, long enough for the example to prove something.

Prove what, though? That was a point of controversy even then. 'This has nothing to do with socialism, it goes against its very substance, its principles, its laws and its whole experience.' Thus its critics, both East and West, speaking in strange unison, their ideas of socialism being astonishingly similar, though the ones worship and the others condemn it. 'Show me a small, non-socialist country without a nationalized film industry where you can find so many creative people, where so many would be given the opportunity to make films and so many would achieve such results!' argued others, in both East and West, whose concept of socialism is exactly opposite to that of the former, for which reason they unite in castigating them for it.

Soviet tanks in the streets of Prague, and the 'normalization' they imposed on the country, gave a convincing answer to both groups. But did they? When it was all over, the British director Lindsay Anderson told me: 'I was always very much on your side, I wrote about Czechoslovak films in the sixties and used them as an example against the jungle of the British film industry. Yet deep in my heart I felt fear and doubt. Subconsciously I could not help feeling that in your case there is no guarantee that it won't all vanish overnight. Without hope. Whereas here there always is some hope. Only ...'

Did the Soviet tanks thus provide the answer on socialism? It might well appear so, and those in the East and West who believe this can, on the face of it, be fairly confident that they are right. Those who think this is not the final word on the subject are considerably worse off.

Where the Czechoslovak film miracle is concerned, the Soviet tanks were undoubtedly right, as were those both in Prague and

Moscow who were certain that the imperial power would not sit idly by and let things go on as they were. What has subsequently happened to those who brought fame to the Czechoslovak film industry in the sixties, to three generations of directors whose names, for a few years at least, became famous the world over?

Many of them left. Away from those tanks, knowing they would not find life in exile easy, but refusing to believe that the tanks would make it any easier.

Martin Frič, the father – or one might say ancestor – of them all, the man who shot the largest number of films in the history of Czech and Slovak cinematography, died the day after the tanks arrived. He gave up his struggle against illness, lost the will to live.

The second of the famous film-makers of the thirties, Otakar Vávra, remained true to himself. A member of the pre-war Czech Left and one of its spokesmen, Vávra continued to work during the Nazi occupation, avoiding jail, concentration camp and the guillotine which took the toll of so many of his close friends and associates. He made six films during the war years 1939–45. After the war he became a leading representative of the Czech nationalized film industry, and in the worst Stalinist years in the fifties was chairman of the so-called Artistic Council. It was then that he shot his worst film, *Into Battle*, and his Hussite trilogy, all four pictures being examples of the worst products of Czech Stalinist socialist realism. In the sixties he underwent yet another change of heart, his *Romance for Trumpet* and *Golden Rennet* belonging to the best films made by members of his generation in that particular period. During the so-called 'Prague Spring' he was one of the most outspoken critics of the former regime. In 1970 he was the first, and indeed the only, leading Czechoslovak film-maker to sign a declaration of loyalty to the Husák regime, after which he turned his hand to two super-productions dealing with recent Czechoslovak history – about the Munich *diktat*, and Sokolovo which tells the story of the Czechoslovak forces in the USSR during the last war.

Jiří Weiss, the most promising of the young pre-war talents, launched his film career in England during the war. Refusing offers to stay in London, where he could have become a successful British director, he returned home to help realise his old dream of a nationalized film industry. In 1969, having had a highly successful career and won a number of international prizes, he emigrated, first to Britain and then to the USA, where he now teaches at the City University of New York.

Another member of that generation, Jiří Krejčík, the director of *Conscience* and *Moral Principle*, remained in Prague. A rebel by nature and a tireless fighter for better conditions within the nationalized film industry, he made his last film in 1970, when he was allowed to finish his version of the Boccaccio stories for which he had written a screenplay some time earlier. Since then nothing, except the odd television job.

Ivan Passer and Miloš Forman emigrated after the 1968 invasion. They have both found success in the USA, where Passer has now made three films – *Born to Win* with George Segal and Karen Black, *Law and Disorder* with Ernest Borgnine, Carrol O'Connor and Karen Black, and *Ace Up My Sleeve* with Omar Sharif and Karen Black. Miloš Forman made a successful American debut with his *Taking Off* and went on to create, in 1975, one of the best American films of recent years, *One Flew Over the Cuckoo's Nest*, with Jack Nicholson and Louise Fletcher, the only film to win five major Oscars since Frank Capra's *It Happened One Night* over thirty years ago.

Jaroslav Papoušek the last member of the trio, who had been co-author of the screenplays of Passer's and Forman's Czech pictures, remained at home. He followed his first directorial effort, *The Most Beautiful Age*, with a trilogy about the family of Prague taxi-driver Homolka, a satire on the Czech petit bourgeois. However, his enchanting humour has grown somewhat ponderous, and he has not made any new films in the last few years. Vojtěch Jasny, one of the leading members of the middle generation, creator of the unforgettable *All My Fellow-Countrymen*, which has been banned 'forever' by the post-invasion regime, only emigrated in 1970 when, as he put it, he had exhausted all the possibilities to work at home. He lives in Salzburg and teaches at the Austrian Film School; in 1975 he filmed Heinrich Böll's *Diary of a Clown* in West Germany.

The originator of the Laterna Magica and a leading Czech stage producer, director of the innovatory film *The Long Voyage*, banned immediately on completion in 1948, Alfred Radok, worked after 1969 as a producer in the Municipal Theatre in Göteborg (Sweden). He died suddenly, while on a visit to Vienna, in April 1976.

The Slovak director Stanislav Barabáš is working in German and Swedish television, continuing his series of films based on subjects taken from Dostoyevsky and Strindberg, which he began in Bratislava with his successful film version of *The Gentle One*.

Jan Kadár, co-director of *Shop on Main Street*, which won a Hollywood Oscar, now lives in the USA, where he has made two feature films: *Angel Levine* based on a story by Bernard Malamud, with Zero Mostel and Harry Belafonte as its stars, and the commercially very successful *Lies My Father Told Me*. Kadár teaches film direction at the school of the American Film Institute in Los Angeles.

Until last year the Director of this school was yet another Czech film director, the former Dean of the Prague Film Faculty, František Daniel, who now holds a professorship at a university in Minnesota.

These exiles were joined in 1974 by Jan Němec, author of *Diamonds of the Night, Martyrs of Love* and *The Party and the Guests*. He has since made three films in West Germany and Switzerland, the latest of these being *Metamorphosis*, based on Franz Kafka. The same story was most successfully used in Sweden by the young Czech director I. Dvořák, whose career in fact only started in exile.

The documentary film-maker, laureate of the Golden Lion of the Venice Film Festival, Václav Táborsky, is a professor in Kitchener, Canada. Another two Czech exiles in that country are the cameraman František Valert and the actor and screenwriter Vladimír Valenta of *The Defendant* and *Closely Watched Trains* – who had been appointed head of the screenwriting department of feature shorts at the National Film Board of Canada. The best Slovak cameraman, Igor Luther, who worked with Juraj Jakubisko, is now active in West Germany.

Worst hit of those who stayed in Czechoslovakia has been Pavel Juráček. His last film, *Case for a Rookie Hangman*, which was made in 1969, was banned after a short run on a limited distribution circuit, and the author of *Josef Kilian* has now spent six years without work. The same goes for Věra Chytilová, who had not, until 1976, even been allowed to make children's films or to work abroad. Director Evald Schorm has also not been given an opportunity to work on films since 1969, but he can produce drama and opera in provincial theatres. Elmar Klos, Jan Kadár's co-director on the Oscar-winning *Shop on Main Street* and other films, has been forced to give up his post as professor at the Prague Film School and cannot work in the industry.

Of the other well-known directors, Karel Kachyna is making films for children. He has recently been joined in the genre by Hynek Bočan and František Vláčil, both of whom have had a long enforced break. Ladislav Helge, the last General Secretary of the disbanded Union of Film and TV Workers and author of a number of politically audacious films of the fifties and sixties, is working behind the counter at a Post Office, while Luděk Pacovsky, another former secretary of the Union, has been driving a taxi since 1969.

The youngest film-makers, who scarcely managed to make their debut in 1968–9 (Vachek, Vihanová, Tuček, Renč and others) have completely vanished from the scene.

Zbyněk Brynych (*Transport from Paradise* and *The Fifth Rider is Fear*) spent a short time in West Germany but then returned to Barrandov where he continues to work. None of his recent films has, however, created any international interest. Jaromil Jireš made two interesting pictures in 1970-1 (*Valerie* and *Give My Love to the Swallows*), of which especially the first, based on an earlier screenplay, was a remarkable tribute to the tradition of Czech surrealism. In 1974 Jireš made *People of the Metro* a film about which the less said the better; it has nothing in common with his previous *oeuvre*, testifying to the violation of a considerable talent.

Who Seeks the Crock of Gold, the first film made since 1969, when his *Lark on a String* was banned before it could be shown, by the creator of *Closely Watched Trains*, Jiří Menzel, proved a complete flop at the Berlin Festival. It is quite possible, though, that Menzel, who earned the right to return to Barrandov by publishing an interview in which he condemned his earlier work and that of his friends, will yet find a way to express his ostentatiously uncommitted artistic personality.

The situation in Slovakia is not much better. Here, too, the scene is dominated by third- and fourth-rate directors, who for the most part keep up an endless flow of war and guerrilla pictures. Of the better known ones only Štefan Uher has been able to carry on working, mostly on children's films. The most talented Slovak film-maker, Juraj Jakubisko, has in the last five years only been permitted to make a single documentary – about the construction of an international gas pipeline. Another great talent, Elo Havetta, died last year. And a third member of the younger Slovak directors, who won the first prize at the Mannheim Film Festival in 1969, Dušan Hanák, has only shot one short film – about the painter of strange, poetic pictures who, in the thirties, set off into the mountains and was never seen again.

What, then, is being filmed? After all, Czechoslovakia has made some 150 full-length feature films since the Soviet occupation in 1968. Is it possible that none of these is worth mentioning?

I fear that that is exactly how it is. Every attempt at even the slightest originality is stifled at the screenplay stage, and the studio maintains a vigilant eye during the shooting to ensure that the style of the film remains faithful to the very worst traditions, now almost universally rejected throughout Eastern Europe with the sole exception of some Soviet films. Nothing that shows even a glimmer of talent or the least sign of nonconformity is allowed to pass. Why should this be so? What political motivation can there be for so consistent a suppression of artistic individuality?

The answer is a simple one; it does not apply only to film making and is well known in Czechoslovakia from the time of the Nazi occupation. By the removal of talented people for political reasons (or racial reasons during the war and later class reasons in the fifties) an opportunity has been given to those without talent who had long before either lost out in competition with their more capable colleagues or who had never managed to get their films made at all. These people know only too well that their star will shine only as long as they prevent the talented ones from working. They can only be successful directors (screenwriters, cameramen, actors) as long as the talented directors are unable to direct, screenwriters write, cameramen wield their cameras, etc. As a result, these 'artists' are the most devoted guardians of 'ideological purity', in whose name they are turning the entire Czech and Slovak culture into a desert of talentless conformity.

Cinema Censorship in Brazil

Ian Bruce

During the Geisel administration from March 1974 to March 1979, the Censorship Service of the Federal Police Department banned 47 films, as compared with 117 plays, 400 books, and 840 songs. Although exact figures are hard to come by, this represents something like 1.7 per cent of all new films, roughly 10 per cent of new plays and 0.8 per cent of new books.

However, such statistics are misleading. Censorship is just one of the devices used by the authorities to control cultural activities they consider potentially dangerous. To get a comprehensive picture, we must see how film production and distribution are organized, what kind of films can be produced, by whom, and for what kind of public. The greater the official control of cultural production, the less need to police its consumption.

Cinema was established in Brazil in the last years of the nineteenth century, before any other medium except the press, which has always catered for a much smaller, élite public. With 250 million tickets sold each year, Brazil today has the largest cinema audience in the Third World outside Asia, and the fifth largest in the Western world as a whole. Brazil's is one of the very few film markets that has continued to sustain economic growth despite the advent of television. But, like wealth, the cinema audience has become concentrated in the industrialized south-east. (The states of São Paulo and Rio de Janeiro alone, with 29 per cent of the country's population, account for 56 per cent of the total declared box-office takings.) The audience is made up largely of the rich, the middle classes, and some better-off members of the working class. The consumers of Brazil's new consumer society.

At least since 1912, when the international monopolies first began to move in, and more systematically since the creation in 1946 of the Motion Pictures Association of America, this market has been dominated by foreign films, imported chiefly from the United States. Exhibition, and until very recently all distribution, has been firmly in the hands of foreign capital. In 1976, when the production of Brazilian films reached the record figure of 85, making it one of the biggest film industries in the world, 482 foreign pictures were imported; the total number of foreign movies being shown, including older ones doing the rounds, was about 4,000. (The USA, with an audience eight times that of Brazil's puts only about 500 films on its home market each year.) As a result, those Brazilian films which do get made have enormous difficulties in finding exhibition outlets. From the exhibitors' point of view, the economic rationale is clear: a foreign film arriving in Brazil has already paid off its production costs and will need to make up only the cost of printing extra copies and putting them on the market – about US$80,000. A Brazilian film, on the other hand, has to pay off *all* the costs, amounting to some US$200,000.

For most Brazilians, then, film culture is imported culture. Hollywood super-productions reach all sectors of the market. Always allowing for some overlap, these are supplemented by European art movies for the economic and cultural élites, B-type adventure and pulp for the middle classes, and a dose of Kung-Fu for the lower echelons.

Legislation

It is only in the light of this domination by international interests that the policies of control adopted by successive Brazilian regimes begin to take on their true significance. State intervention falls into three categories:

1. Economic and institutional measures to influence production, distribution, and exhibition.
2. Propaganda initiatives such as compulsory exhibition of government-sponsored newsreels and the like.
3. Censorship of finished films.

Of these, the first is the most important. Characteristically, it has been combined with the others in a variable formula which pits timid gestures of economic nationalism against a recognition of overriding global dependence, the whole precarious package being wrapped in a protective mantle of repressive authoritarianism.

A look at the history of cinema legislation in Brazil reveals how censorship and policies to 'protect' home production were born under the same star. In 1932, the first law to institute prior censorship of films on a national scale (under the direction of the then Ministry of Education and Health) was also the first to suggest reserving exhibition time for Brazilian films. In 1939, under the populist dictatorship of Getulio Vargas, the control of all press and propaganda activities, including cinema, was passed to the Department of Press and Propaganda (DIP), which not only laid down many of the censorship norms still operative today, but also introduced the first, albeit ridiculously inadequate, protectionist measure: the compulsory exhibition by every cinema of at least one Brazilian feature film per annum. (By 1945 nearly 20 were being made every year.)

On 24 January 1946 came the law which still governs film censorship. Inheriting much of the repressive machinery of Vargas's DIP, the Public Entertainments Censorship Service (SCDP) was created as an organ of the Federal Department of Public Security (now the Federal Police Department - DPF), itself answerable to the Ministry of Justice. Art and culture thus became matters of 'public security'. The mechanisms and categories of censorship are defined. All films and publicity materials are to be submitted for examination by the censors prior to exhibition; certificates of approval are valid for five years only, and then re-examination is obligatory; scenes can be cut; films can be declared inappropriate for exhibition to those under 10, 14, or 18 years of age, or inappropriate for exhibition in certain parts of the country, or inappropriate for export, or simply inappropriate for exhibition, in which case all existing copies of the film shall be confiscated. The law also continues the tradition of treating censorship and commercial control as one single legislative area.

Regulations of the Public Entertainments Censorship Service

Decree No. 20 493 (24 January 1946), Article 41:
Authorisation for presentation, exhibition or radiophonic transmission will not be given when material
(a) contains anything offensive to public decorum
(b) contains scenes of violence or is capable of encouraging criminal acts
(c) gives rise to, or induces, evil habits
(d) is capable of provoking incitement against the existing regime, public order, the authorities, or their agents
(e) might prejudice cordial relations with other countries
(f) is offensive to any community or religion
(g) in any way prejudices national dignity or interests
(h) brings the armed forces into disrepute

After 1946 the commercial stimulation and protection of films was studied and debated at a number of important congresses, which in turn led to the formation of a series of working groups and advisory committees operating under the aegis of the Ministry of Education in the late fifties and early sixties; and these finally led to the setting up of a National Cinema Institute (INC) in 1966.

All the legislative and institutional measures of the state during this long period have the same function, irrespective of the declared ideology of the government responsible. Whilst appearing to favour the home product, and in fact gradually increasing the period reserved for it each year from seven days in 1939 to 84 days in 1969, they underwrite the international cinema monopolies' control of the market by refusing to tackle the two key issues of any serious protectionist policy: investment in home production, and import controls. The dominant presence of foreign films is taken for granted, and the Brazilian film's role defined as that of an ailing competitor with this mightier imported counterpart. It was only in the seventies, with the appearance of a new state enterprise, Embrafilme, to provide production finance and organize the distribution of Brazilian films, with 123 days per year allotted to them, and legislation on the inclusion of one Brazilian short in the programme alongside every imported feature, that the first genuine attempt was made to win back the home market.

However, the Brazilian market is still dominated by imported films, and the same foreign domination is, if anything, even more firmly entrenched in the now more important medium of television. Nevertheless, new and more subtle forms of ideological control are now being tried.

'Cinema novo'

But the taming of Brazilian cinema is not entirely without obstacles. There have been, and still are, elements of resistance which have to be suppressed.

To understand these we must return to the early sixties, from a cultural point of view to the most vital moment in the history of Brazilian cinema. It was then that the movement we have come to know as 'cinema novo' – the films which were mainly responsible for establishing a reputation for Brazilian cinema abroad – appeared as something insignificant. This very insignificance was the movement's great strength, but also the source of its vulnerability. Financed privately by some of the most progressive sectors of the national bourgeoisie and propelled by middle-class intellectuals, its objective was to establish a process of popular communication, taking a radical view of Brazilian reality through the elaboration of a peculiarly national cinematic language. Strong on rhetoric and aesthetics, but weak on organised penetration of the popular classes it intended to reach, 'cinema novo' was suppressed after 1964 with the same ease as other expressions of the popular movement.

Towards the end of the sixties, as political tensions mounted once again, personal intimidation was used more extensively to curtail film-making activities which refused to conform to the prescribed norms. The following are examples:

1. **Gilberto Machado** Assistant director of Glauber Rocha's *Deus e o Diabo na Terra do Sol* ('Black God, White Devil') and of various shorts. Arrested but subsequently released as a result of international pressure. Forced into exile.

2. **Alney Sao Paulo** Arrested in connection with his film *Manha Cinzenta* ('Grey Morning'), made during the student demonstrations in 1968. Spent one month in prison, under almost continuous psychological torture. On release had to spend two months in a psychiatric clinic undergoing treatment for insomnia. The others involved in the film were also harassed, and the film is still banned.

3. **Ronaldo Duarte** Documentary film-maker. He and his brother Rogerio Duarte, a graphic artist responsible for designing many 'cinema novo' film posters, were detained for two months without anyone knowing their whereabouts. Underwent various forms of torture, including electric shock treatment and the 'parrot's perch'.

4. **Sergio Sanz** Documentary film-maker. Spent one month undergoing continuous interrogation, as a result of which he had to be treated in a psychiatric clinic. He was actually arrested because the police could not find his brother ...

5. **Luis Alberto Sanz** Condemned, but fled into exile. In Sweden he made, with Noilton Nutes, *Leucemia*, a film about the suicide in Paris of a young Brazilian girl released (but banished) in exchange for the release of a kidnapped diplomat. The film remains banned in Brazil.

6. **Cosme Alves Neto** Director of the Cinemathéque of the Museum of Modern Art in Rio de Janeiro. Accused, without any evidence, of participating in a bank hold-up, and held in prison for two-and-a-half months. Submitted to various tortures, he was made to sit in a cell filled with freezing water.

7. **Plinio Sussekind da Rocha** Lecturer in astronomy and director of the film library of the University of Rio de Janeiro. Spent three weeks in prison for possessing copies of Einsenstein's *Battleship Potemkin* and

Pudovkin's *The Mother*. These, the best copies in Brazil, were confiscated, and remain among the classics of world cinema still banned in Brazil. Plinio, who was in his sixties at the time of his arrest, was banned from teaching and experienced considerable hardship.

Other, and perhaps better-known representatives of 'cinema novo', also suffered. Joaquim Pedro de Andrade was accused of holding subversive meetings in his house and spent four days in detention; Neville d'Almeida and Carlos ('Caca') Diegues, who have since taken up Embrafilme's commercial banner with such soft-porn features as *Dama do Lotacdo* ('The Lady on the Bus') and *Xica da Silva*, had their flats raided or were summonsed to make statements; Walter Lima Junior was held for weeks without charges being brought, and was tortured; the leading film critic, Jean-Claude Bernadet, was dismissed from his teaching posts at the universities of Brasilia and São Paulo.

Censorship in action

All these developments have meant that the area over which censorship has had to act has been reduced to a minimum. Some of the best 'cinema novo' film-makers have still managed to make acute metaphorical statements about present-day social and political conditions by using literary and historical adaptation. Consequently, films like *Macunaima, Como Era Gostoso o meu Frances* ('How Tasty Was My Little Frenchman'), *Os Inconfidentes* ('The Rebels'), and *São Bernardo*, along with many others, have suffered cuts or delays. But the most savage censorship has been reserved for those 'marginal' areas of filmmaking whose practitioners rejected compromise and continued with the original political and aesthetic projects of the early sixties.

The case of Vladimir Carvalho's feature-length documentary about the settlement of the depressed north-eastern backlands, *O Pais de São Sarue*, is a good example. Begun in 1966 with meagre resources (Carvalho produced the film on his own, to avoid any outside interference with his project), a preliminary 16mm version was shown at the Museum of Modern Art and the Maison de France in Rio de Janeiro two years later.

'The warm welcome it received encouraged me to continue, at considerable personal sacrifice,' said Vladimir Carvalho in a statement for this issue of *Index*, 'until in 1971 I had the definitive 35mm version ready for screening in accordance with the norms imposed by the market. In other words, I could now show it to the general public, take it to the north-east and discuss it with the people who had helped me make it as the actors in the drama of their own poverty.'

But with the Médici government recently installed and repression in full swing, the time was hardly propitious for a film dealing with the agrarian problem which had been a major factor in sparking off the 1964 military coup. In October 1971 the film was unconditionally banned from exhibition in Brazil and abroad as 'injurious to the national dignity and interest'.

Vladimir decided to wait for another opportunity, which came with the Brasilia Film Festival. 'I entered the film, knowing that it was usual practice for the Brasilia Cultural Foundation, which organizes the Festival, to intercede with the censors on behalf of the selected films, getting them passed irrespective of whether they had been banned or cut.'

The film was chosen by the selection committee to compete for the main prize, but the Foundation, conscious of the prevailing political climate, decided not to intercede that year. Not only did they not ratify the choice of Carvalho's film, but themselves proposed a substitute: the semi-propaganda picture, *Brasil, Bom de Bola* ('Brazil, Good with the Ball'), a tribute to the national team's successes in the Mexico World Cup. The selection committee published a protest in the press, and this was followed by another protest organized by Paulo Emilio Salles Gomes, author of the standard work on Jean Vigo – but the damage was done. Emilo Fontana's *Nenen Bandalho* ('Baby Bandalho') was also dropped from the Festival on the grounds that it encouraged drug-taking and showed disrespect to the police.

'I also recall an episode which may serve to illustrate the methods of Brazil's censors,' Vladimir Carvalho told *Index*. 'As soon as I realized that I was on my own, I, perhaps naïvely, went to the Censorship Service and asked to see its head, Rogerio Numes, to make one more plea for the film to be released just for the Festival. He received me with apparent concern and sent for the relevant files. Then he told me that he was about to see General Canepa, the Director of the Federal Police, and that he would consult him on the matter. Nearly two hours later, at the very end of the day, he came back and confidentially drew me aside and told me that the General had spoken to the Minister of Justice, Alfredo Buzaid, who had recommended that the film not be shown at the Festival as it might provoke polemics which would be damaging to the government at that moment. Not much used to this kind of contact with the corridors of power (and much less with those of police departments), I left, depressed and astonished. After all, judging by what he had said, even a minister of state was worried about the consequences of my work. Looking back on the incident today, I realise I must have been extraordinarily naïve to believe "Dr Rogerio" and I understand why that always elegant, amenable and adroit man has been such a success at the head of the Censorship Service. Minister Buzaid had probably never even heard of *São Sarue*.'

The Brasilia Film Festival was shelved in 1972, 1973 and 1974. For the government, it was clearly inconvenient to have such a conspicuous forum for debate which could only cause them worry and expense. The film *São Sarue* was invited to participate in the festivals of Leipzig, Cannes, and Mannheim, and on each occasion Vladimir requested the Censorship Service to reconsider its decision. 'I believe it was this persistence, together with continuous references to the film in the press, which helped to keep it a live issue and which culminated in its eventual release in January 1979 as part of the general climate of 'distensão' (political relaxation). But what most delighted me was the fact that this happened at a historic moment, when all the country was clamouring for a return to the rule of law, to political and institutional normality. That's to say, it was not a question of any personal intervention; no strings were pulled or private agreements reached to pass the film. It was carried through on the wave of a general pressure for democracy. We must be sure not to accept it as an isolated case, as a cosmetic trick to show off the regime's generosity. It's absolutely essential that it should be followed by the release of many other works in the various arts, in music, the theatre, literature, and the media.'

This case study underlines two important aspects of current film censorship in Brazil. Festivals have become one of the only remaining outlets for those film-makers who continue to explore more politically sensitive material and more progressive film techniques. For the same reason censorship has clamped down harder on the festivals. Many films entered in festivals have been vetoed by the censors and the festival organizers have taken it upon themselves to vet the programmes. Sometimes, fearing the embarrassment of confrontation with the producers and their public, they have resorted to less obvious subterfuges, such as providing inadequate screening conditions, insufficient seating, muddled schedules, or non-existent publicity.

Secondly, there is the 'reality criterion' which Vladimir Carvalho believes singles out documentary cinema for sterner repression. Some such yardstick has indeed been employed since 1964. The retreat of much 'cinema novo' into metaphor and mysticism has already been mentioned. Yet, 35mm feature films which cut just too close to the bone still appear occasionally.

This even happens with those versions of famous literary works so cherished by the state apparatus. Witness the example of Zelito Vianna's *Morte e Vida Severina*, based on Joa Cabral de Melo Neto's fine dramatic poem of the same name, which was awarded the National Council of Brazilian Bishops' 'Silver Daisy' as the best new film of 1977. Taking up the cinema novo's pet theme of poverty in the north-east, it combines deliberately stylized routines of musical drama with documentary sequences showing the miserable living conditions. It was presumably these scenes the censors deemed 'dishonourable to Brazil', declaring the film unsuitable for exportation.

Jorge Bodansky's *Iracema* uses a cinema vérité style of synchronous sound, sweeping hand-held camera movements and non-professional actors to trace the peregrinations of a young half-Indian prostitute through the periphery of the Amazonian forest, where wholesale devastation, exploitation, and 'white slavery' are the fruits of insatiable industrial expansion and an official policy of colonialization, intended to defuse the explosive misery of the north-east. The film was shot in 1974 and processed in West Germany because at that time there were no facilities in Brazil for developing the kind of negative used. The powers that be took advantage of this and denied the film a certificate of Brazilian nationality. The censors said they could consider the film only if it were presented with the certificate of nationality. CONCINE (the successor to INC, and now effectively an organ of Embrafilme) said they would issue the certificate only if the film were passed by the censors. Stalemate. Finally, in 1978, Bodansky received a written declaration from the Censorship Service that the film's 'non-release was upheld'; which presumably meant that it had been censored. In any case, the film, shown on West German television, still remains unseen by the Brazilian public. Another film of Bodansky's, *Gitirana*, has also been banned since 1975, and for both cases his explanation is similar to Vladimir Carvalho's: 'The simple, unvarnished truth contained in them.'

When Luis Rosemberg's *Asuntina das Americas* was finally banned in 1977, the censors were merely formalizing a two-year boycott put into effect by Embrafilme. Once the working copy was ready, Embrafilme had agreed to provide the money to cut it and put on the soundtrack. This was done by the usual process of buying the distribution rights in advance. The film then sat on Embrafilme's shelves for two years before the Federal Police kindly took it off their hands. Here the criterion was not one of 'documentary realism'; rather it was a question of inconvenient issues being raised by a cinematic language which fitted none of the ratified genres. In iconoclastic style, the film attempts to rethink the history of Brazilian cinema itself, and its relation to the social context; the final segment confronts directly the relationship between Embrafilme and the concept of cinema as big business. The same tactic of cold storage has been applied to many other 'unwholesome commodities'.

Inconvenient films do still get released, however, and then the authorities have to invoke their powers of regulating distribution. *Ladroes de Cinema* ('Cinema Thieves') is one of the very few recent Brazilian films which, despite all the obstacles, has made a real advance in the development of an authentically popular national film language. To some extent following up the lead set by Nelson Pereira in *Amuleto de Ogum*, it takes one of the authorized commercial genres (in this case the historical spectacle) and delivers it into the hands of the people – a shanty town community staging and filming for their own benefit an utterly self-conscious, and hysterically funny, account of Tiradentes' rebellion against the Portuguese. Although hugely applauded at the 1977 Brasilia festival, the film was distributed hurriedly and almost without publicity, on the grounds that it was too difficult for the public to understand. A similar fate befell Ruy Guerra and Nelson Xavier's *A Queda* ('The Fall'), one of the first serious attempts at treating an urban working-class (as opposed to lumpenproletariat) theme. Here the reputation of the directors and cast, combined with the Silver Bear from the 1978 Berlin Festival, made any crude policy of boycott impracticable. The film was given a full accolade and distributed in some of the best cinemas in Rio's affluent southern districts. But by a strange stroke of misfortune, the dates fixed for exhibition in Rio's working-class northern zone fell through. The workers, with whom and for whom the film was made, thus missed it. At the same time no expense is spared to turn the carnivalesque populism and soft porn of films like *Xica da Silva*, *Dona Flor e seus dois Maridos* or *A Dama do Lotacao* into enormous box-office successes.

Foreign films

The censorship of foreign films has not been mentioned because it is largely a side issue. With the import business wholly in the hands of the international monopolies, censorship only needs to be exercised against a small number of 'prestige' political productions such as films of the Costa Gavras *State of Siege* type, or against those international 'pornographic' films which, unlike the Brazilian state-sponsored 'pornochanchadas', use sex in a way that is felt to threaten the male-dominated, family-centred principles of the military's much vaunted last bastion of Western Christendom.

Much more important than this phenomenon, or even than the removal from circulation after 1964 of numerous classics of world political cinema (early Soviet examples have already been mentioned, though it is interesting to note that Eisenstein's 'Stalinist' films, from *Alexander Nevsky* on, are not forbidden), is the impossibility of maintaining contact with the most vital currents in contemporary world cinema. Not as a result of direct censorship, but rather of import monopoly, Straub, all late Godard, and most Pasolini are absent. Yet at a time when Embrafilme itself is working hard to move into the export markets offered by the Spanish and Portuguese speaking world, the total absence of major Latin American and African films is an even graver lack. Brazilian film-makers themselves, unless they are widely travelled, have almost certainly never seen the work of Sanjines, Littin, Solanas, or Sembene, much less the major films of Cuban or Arab cinema. An isolated exception was the São Paulo International Season, which last year showed for the first time a Cuban film, Alea's *The Last Supper*, which won the top award. When the festival moved to Brasilia, Alea's film was dropped. The local journalists' union then decided to show the film. The first performance had an enthusiastic audience filling every inch of standing room, with many more left outside. On the second evening the cinema had mysteriously closed. A number of painfully obvious plainclothes policemen stood around, and the security guard informed disappointed members of the public that the projectors had unfortunately broken down.

Commodity versus culture
Fifteen years of slowly diminishing police repression and steadily mounting industrial control have mutilated an already distorted and colonized film culture. Straining to occupy a little of the space shaped and still ambiguously guarded by 'Mister' Jack Valenti's Hollywood dragons, 'film as commodity' has supplanted 'film as culture'.

The rigid interpretation of the five-year validity of censorship certificates is both a symptom and an aggravation of this consumer ethos. Every year the copies of some 700 'obsolete' films are chopped up and cremated. In 1978 these included such important films of the early seventies as *Vai Trabalhar Vagabundo*, *Joanna Francesa* and *Compasso de Espera*. Cinema novo itself has been quietly erased. With the exception of very occasional and incomplete retrospective screenings for privileged connoisseur audiences, it is virtually impossible to see the major Brazilian films of the sixties or earlier. In fact of many of them, including *Os Fuzis* ('The Guns') and *Deus e o Diabo na Terra do Sol* ('Black God, White Devil'), not a single complete copy seems to exist in the country.

And yet the most important personalities in Brazilian cinema continue to resist, even though part of their strategy may be dubious.

The space opened up by the state's industrial intervention is carrying in its wake as yet confused and sporadic attempts to revive a genuinely popular national cinema. It must be hoped that the massive pressure for democratization, and initiatives like those of the new film-makers' cooperative in Rio, will give these attempts a more solid basis than they have had in the past.

Rebirth of Chilean Cinema

Malcolm Coad

- On 16 August 1977 a group of Chilean film-makers wrote an open letter to the military government's Secretary for Cultural Relations. They were asking for state aid to be given to cinema. In the letter they said: 'Cinema is doomed to die here very soon.'
- In the first week of January 1979 the only film school left open in Chile after the military coup of September 1973 closed its doors indefinitely. Its director said that it was unclear whether it was necessary to train more students. One of the last seven students said: 'Last year they censored five of our films – films which are eight or ten minutes long. One had a nude man in it and another a conflict about unemployment. We asked for clear instructions about what we could film. They said, "no violence, no sex and no poverty".'
- Towards the end of April 1979 Silvio Caiozzi's film *Julio Comienza en Julio* ('Julio Begins in July') opened in Santiago. It was the first feature film to be made and shown in Chile since the coup. It was shot in black-and-white and 16mm to keep the costs down and took three years to make and edit, work on it being held up several times for lack of money.
- Meanwhile, in the same month, exiled Chilean director Miguel Littín's latest film was showing in five Paris cinemas simultaneously. It is a Franco-Mexican-Cuban co-production called *Viva el Presidente*, based on *El Recurso del Metodo* ('Reasons of State'). Alejo Carpentier's novel about an anonymous Latin American military dictator. It is the latest of the 21 features, 11 medium length shorts and 21 shorts which have been made or completed by exiled Chilean film-makers since the coup.

Vol. 5, no. 2, 1980

These facts eloquently record the progress of Chilean cinema since 11 September 1973. Between them, the military dictatorship and the determination of Chilean film-makers have produced a phenomenon which is unique in the history of cinema: an energetic and self-consciously national cinema whose main centres of activity are located outside its borders. When the Chilean writer Ariel Dorfman wrote in late 1977 of 'the culture that is going into exile on a mass scale', he described what was taking place as 'a matter of preserving the national identity somewhere, anywhere, of keeping alive the consciousness and colours of Chile, of cultivating roots in tiny plots of ground which will one day become common ground'. Chilean cinema in exile has begun to extend those plots. And, in Chile itself, where the military have almost fatally crippled film-making, the tiniest of roots still continue to spring up. For the military junta all this is nastily ironic, providing further confirmation of the malevolence of a decadent world. An activity which they had done their utmost to destroy, in order to extirpate the 'Marxist cancer' it nurtured, has re-emerged in a dozen corners of the world, guided by the very people they had driven out. For those of us who do not share the junta's view of culture and human life it is confirmation of a different sort – of the fact that it is easy to destroy the tools of a person's trade, but much harder to bury the determination that will send him or her searching for other ones.

The inauguration of this new era in the fraught history of Chilean cinema was abrupt and brutal. Cinema was hit by the military's onslaught in the same way as every other sphere of cultural activity. Every film school, distributor and centre of production in any way connected with the previous government was militarily occupied. At the State Technical University the Department of Cinema's installations were destroyed, its entire film library impounded, its staff sacked. The University of Chile's Department of Cinema and its Cinemateca were closed after most of their staff had been imprisoned or dismissed. Their archives were seized, though not before some of them had been rescued, later to be smuggled out of the country. The installations at the Central Trades Union Confederation's (CUT) Film Department were confiscated and all its archives and film material destroyed. The Cinema, Radio and Television Actors and Technicians Union (SIDARTE) was put under military control, its national and local premises closed and many of its members arrested, imprisoned or, like the president of its Concepción branch, Fernando Alvarez, killed. Some went underground or left the country. Others, like actress Carmen Bueno and cameraman Jorge Müller in 1974 joined the hundreds of disappeared prisoners whose arrests have never been officially admitted. The state production and distribution company, Chile Films, bore the brunt of the repression. Its premises were occupied and its irreplaceable negative archives indiscriminately destroyed, including a priceless collection of the country's earliest newsreels. Its staff were sacked *en bloc*, many being arrested, imprisoned and tortured. Several died, including the director, Eduardo Paredes (who was killed alongside President Allende and Augusto Olivares, the Director of Channel 7 TV, in the Moneda presidential palace), and, some months after the coup, Carlos Arevalo, who had distributed films to trade unions and shanty-town communities, and the cameraman Hugo Araya. Chile Films productions were banned. Film and sound-tapes were burned in the streets together with books, magazines, pamphlets, posters, and university theses. The only film school left more or less functioning, until its closure in 1979, was that of the School of Arts and Communication at the Catholic University. Parts of its premises, however, together with those of Channel 13 TV's Film Institute and the University's Department of Worker and Peasant Education, were burned down in a mysterious fire five weeks after the coup.

Not even the private distributors and local branches of the cinema multinationals, all of them rabid opponents of the Popular Unity government, were left untouched. In accordance with the junta's policy of taking direct charge of every sphere of activity, whether cultural, educational or economic, the directors of these concerns were appointed government 'delegates', thereby becoming equally answerable to the junta as they were to their superiors in New York, Miami and London. But the possibility of any real conflict of interest was purely academic. The Chilean market accounts for a mere 0.5 per cent of the cinema multinationals' income. During the lifetime of the Popular Unity government these companies had imposed a strict boycott on Chile. But now, precisely 22 days after the coup, they were back in Santiago, in the amiable person of Robert Corkery, the Vice-President of the Association of Film Producers of the USA, to discuss the 'new situation'.

Censorship of the mass media, including cinema, has been under the jurisdiction of various bodies since the coup. The basic task of all of them has been, in General Pinochet's words, to 'purify and liberate Chilean thought from the poison of politics'. Immediately after the coup the Military Council for Telecommunications banned all radio and TV programmes 'with content' (sic) and issued the following guidelines: 'Dramatic broadcasts and other programmes of fiction must contain moral concepts which do not damage morality or high principles or exalt morbidity. They may not use the situation of the country as inspiration.' Soon afterwards the *Direccion de Informaciones y Communicaciones Sociales* was set up to oversee all information, cultural and advertising media. Its director was Colonel Virgilio Espinosa, a specialist in military security who, just prior to the coup, had been training at the course of Continental Defense run by the Interamerican Defense Academy in Washington DC. The DICS was later superseded by the *Direccion Nacional de Communicaciones Sociales* (DINACOS), presided over by a series of army colonels. The general quality of this body's thinking can be gathered from its declaration of 10 June 1978 that pornography is a weapon used by the Soviet Union to destroy spiritual health and thereby subvert 'Western Christian society'. In July 1977 this same body had published a lengthy and blustering attack on two Santiago radio stations, accusing them of being in league with foreign powers because they broadcast letters from the relatives of disappeared prisoners.

As far as cinema specifically is concerned the formal adjunct to direct physical repression for the first year after the coup continued to be the *Consejo de Censura Cinematográfica*, which was founded in 1963 and functioned something like the British Board of Film Censors. Article 3 of Decree Law 679, published on 10 October 1974, transformed the *Consejo de Censura* into the *Consejo de Calificación Cinematográfica*, composed of 19 members (in place of the previous seven) including judges, representatives of all the armed forces, journalists, academics and 'fathers of families', under the jurisdiction of the Ministry of Education, which could overrule its decisions. The Consejo's purpose was to operate a 'more modern and effective protection of our cultural and artistic patrimony' by weeding out 'films which foment and propagate doctrines and ideas, such as Marxism and others, which are contrary to the fundamental bases of the fatherland and nation, public order, morality and good habits'. Films banned between 1974 and 1976 included *Fiddler on the Roof* ('contains elements opposed to harmony among Chileans'), *Nicholas and Alexandra*, Costa Gavras' *Section Speciale* and the thriller about a plot to assassinate General de Gaulle *The Day of the Jackal* ('encourages anti-social acts by exalting violence'). In June 1975 a commission was established to propose a definitive body of laws governing cultural activity which would 'permit the country's communications media to act within a framework compatible with the propositions of the government'. On 14 March 1976 this body was declared permanent and given the task of presenting quarterly reports on cultural matters to the ministries of Education and Justice. Supreme Decree no 19 of the

Ministry of Education required that in future 'all initiatives, whether public or private, which relate to cultural activities' should be presented for approval to this commission and to the junta's own cultural assessor.

That the dictatorship should strike so hard against Chilean cinema, and cultural activity in general, is not surprising. For fifteen years Chilean film-makers had been in the forefront of attempts to create a solidly based national and popular culture in opposition to the economic and ideological control from abroad which has been the central fact of Latin American cultural life (and society generally) since the arrival of the *conquistadores*. The very nature of cinema as an art with enormous mass popular appeal, but which, because it requires considerable capital resources, is wide open to control by multinational monopolies, had heightened this militant commitment among Latin American film-makers. Movements developed such as Cinema Novo in Brazil and revolutionary Cuban cinema, all of them identified with the political left. From the late 1960s, the 'new Chilean cinema' clearly took its place among these. It played a central part in the remarkable cultural flowering of the Popular Unity years, when, as director Miguel Littín described at the 1974 meeting of Latin American film-makers in Caracas, Venezuela: 'More novels and essays were published and read, more music recorded, more murals pained, more exhibitions mounted and more theatre and dance companies founded than at any other time in the country's history.' Despite the sluggishness of the organizational apparatus available and the general problems film-makers faced, an unprecedented 13 fictional features, 71 short and long documentaries and 41 newsreels were made, while new distribution channels were set up to take films directly to trades unions, shanty-towns, local communities and open-air meetings.

The coup finished all this, imposing stasis and mediocrity as the norm. With rare and honourable exceptions virtually the only films made in Chile since the coup, apart from commercials, have been newsreels and travelogues of the most banal and derivative kind. These have been sponsored by, for example, military governors and Esso-Chile and have featured landscape, skiing and the family life of generals. A full-length documentary on the supposed horrors of the Popular Unity was announced, but abandoned. A co-production with Spain on the poet Gabriela Mistral was planned for International Women's Year, but collapsed with Franco's death. Chicago-school economic policies, as well as sheer physical repression and censorship, have exacted their toll. The minimal financial aid allowed to film-makers through tax-exemption on imported equipment and a guaranteed return to them of 20 per cent of box-office takings was withdrawn. Chile Films was placed in the charge of two retired generals before being announced as having been sold to the private owner of a chain of cinemas largely specializing in Kung-fu and soft porn, and was finally put in the charge of the government radio station with orders to finance itself. Spiralling inflation was meanwhile placing bus fares to the cinema, never mind the price of admission, beyond the pockets of more and more people. The curfew meant that films had to finish at 7 p.m. The Chilean film 'industry' returned to its traditional role, that of providing raw material to North American and European companies. Sixty years ago this was nitrate, on which the manufacture of film stock used to be based. Now it is landscape and the occasional extra. But even for these there have been few takers.

Despite all the difficulties, however, some film-makers have managed to make films. Silvio Caiozzi, ex-director of photography for two of Chile's best known directors, Helvio Soto and Aldo Francia, has completed or made two features since the coup, financing them from his earnings from commercials. The first, *A la Sombra del Sol* ('In the Shadow of the Sun') was premiered in 1974. The second was *Julio Comienza en Julio*, mentioned above, which began shooting in April 1976. Christian Sanchez has completed *Vias Paralelas* ('Parallel Routes') without being able to obtain distribution for it, and between 1976 and 1979 made the 70-minute long *El zapato chino* ('The Chinese Shoe'). Apart from these features, Carlos Flores and Guillermo Cahn have each made a medium length documentary, both on Chilean writers. Flores's is on Jose Donoso and Cahn's on Nicanor Parra. In many ways the most interesting films made since the coup are a 23-minute short, *Coplas de la Tierra* ('Songs of the Earth'), made in late 1977 by the Ranquil Peasants Confederation with the most rudimentary technical resources and virtually no money; *Delgadino*, a short directed by David Vera-Meiggs and shot in Super-8 in two days in March 1979 with a group of handicraft workers; and *Recado de Chile* ('Message from Chile'), a 20-minute short made clandestinely in 1978. The first of these, which was shown at the 1978 French Festival of Ethnographic and Sociological Film, deals with peasant song, poetry and story-telling traditions. The second, which (significantly) was financed from Europe by the English Folk Song and Dance Society, the Stockholm Ethnographic Museum and Spanish National Radio, is based on a traditional story of seventeenth-century derivation which was collected in the Chilean countryside by the folklorist Gabriela Pizarro, who also appears in the film. The third was made to publicize abroad the sufferings and struggles of the families of the country's thousands of disappeared prisoners. This, then, is the sum total of films made in Chile since 1973 apart from commercials, a fact emphasized by the 13 film-makers grouped in the newly formed Asociacion de Productores de Cine de Chile (Chilean Film Producers Association) at their inaugural press-conference in September 1979.

It is outside Chile, then, that the new Chilean cinema continues to grow, adapting itself to the new context of exile and international solidarity. The film-makers themselves define this cinema as one of resistance, denunciation and the continuing assertion of an authentically popular culture which dictatorships throughout Latin America are systematically attempting to destroy or co-opt. The films made cover almost the entire range of cinematic forms, from full-length features to shorts, narrative fiction to documentary, 'casts-of-thousands' to animation, large-scale productions aided by sympathetic governments and institutions to work financed hand-to-mouth by individuals. Among them are films by Chile's most internationally known directors. In 1974 Miguel Littín completed *La Tierra Prometida* ('The Promised Land'), in which the now disappeared Carmen Bueno is the leading actress. Littín has since made *Actas de Marusia* ('Letters from Marusia'), which was nominated for an Oscar in 1976, and which draws parallels between the 1973 coup and massacres in British-owned nitrate mines in northern Chile at the turn of the century, and *Viva el Presidente*. In 1979 *Poder Popular* ('The Power of the People') was released, the final part of Patricio Guzman's celebrated documentary trilogy *La Batalla de Chile* ('The Battle of Chile'), which was edited in Cuba from material filmed in Chile during the last year before the coup (largely by Jorge Müller, the now long missing cameraman) and smuggled out of the country, and which has already been cited for or won 18 awards at international festivals. Raul Ruiz, director of *Tres Tristes Tigres* ('The Three Sad Tigers') had made no less than eight features and shorts at the last count. Helvio Soto made *Llueve sobre Santiago* ('Rain over Santiago') – the phrase used by supporters of the Left to indicate that the coup had begun) in 1975, a Franco-Bulgarian co-production with Jean-Louis Trintignant, Annie Girardot and Bibi Andersson. Gaston Ancelovici and Orlando Lübbert finished their documentary history of the Chilean labour movement, *Puños frente al Cañon* ('Fists Before the Cannon'), in West Germany, and went on to make a fictional feature *El Paso* ('The Passage') about the escape of a group of Chileans over the Andes. A short, *A los Pueblos del Mundo* ('To the People of the World'), was made in the USA with Carmen Castillo, who was released by the junta after international pressure, and Laura Allende, President Allende's sister. Pablo de la Barra's *Queridos*

Compañeros ('Dear Comrades') was finished in Venezuela, and Sergio Castilla has just made a feature, *Presos Desaparecidos* ('Disappeared Prisoners') in Cuba, his fifth film made in exile there and in Sweden, Patricio Castilla has made two films, Sebastian Alarcon three, and directors such as Claudio Sapiain, Percy Matas and Douglas Hubner several between them. All this work is being archived and publicized by the *Cinemateca Chilena en el Exilio* (Padre Xifre 3, oficina 111, Madrid 2), which was set up with the support of the International Federation of Film Archives to continue the work of the Cinemateca Universitaria, closed by the military after the coup. The Cinemateca also has a unique collection of films rescued from the military and smuggled out of the country.

Exile is the hardest of countries to live in. It can easily bring the loss of a sense of direction, the difficulties of balancing loyalty to homeland with immediate demands, the sterility of endless homage to the past and plain black depression. But Chilean film-makers are image-makers of a continent and half the world. There is a great deal of material yet to be fashioned into the weapons they consider their films to be. And, in the words of Pedro Chaskel, the exiled editor of *The Battle of Chile*:

> Chilean cinema is alive. Everything we've done, all the new expressive possibilities we've discovered, all the experience and maturity we've accumulated will find their full realisation when, sooner or later, they are rooted once again in the reality of Chile and in the new culture which its people are forging from their daily struggle of resistance, their organisation and their unity.

Hooray for Hollywood?

Alan Stanbrook

With a cheap pen and a clutch of exercise books, anybody can write a novel. It may not be published, but anybody can write it. Paints and a canvas are all you need to make a picture. To make and market a film takes, on average, sixteen-and-a-half million dollars. No individual has that kind of money to spare so, if he wants to shoot a film, he has to secure financial backing from one of the leading distributors, known in the film industry as 'the majors'.

There are six of these. Four of them are or have been subsidiaries of giant and wealthy conglomerates. United Artists belonged to Transamerica Corporation, Universal is part of MCA, Warner Bros. is an offshoot of Warner Communications, and Paramount is under the umbrella of Gulf + Western Industries. Only Twentieth Century Fox and Columbia are not linked to conglomerates, though Fox has recently been taken over by the tycoon Marvin Davis. The once great MGM has made few films in recent years but is stepping up production again and is in the process of acquiring United Artists from Transamerica.

Financial domination

The financial domination of the majors means that, at the end of the day, they call the shots. They provide the money for a film, it is their product (not the director's), and they reserve the right to exploit it as they think best. In principle, there is nothing wrong with this. A publisher and his editors exercise much the same rights – often to a book's benefit. In practice, front office interference seldom improves a film because the meddlers are unimaginative men frightened of originality. Their jobs depend on a run of hits, and the best way to ensure that is to imitate previous hits.

Vol. 10, no. 4, 1981

This accounts for all the ersatz *Star Wars* with which screens have been flooded in the past four years. By a miracle of genetic engineering, Fox even managed to cross-breed *Star Wars* with *Jaws* to produce *Alien* (a man-eater in a space-age location). This want of courage creates a form of insidious censorship even before a film is made. One notable film, for example, that could not be made today is Billy Wilder's *Ace in the Hole*. The plot (about an unscrupulous journalist's attempts to spin out a rescue in order to prolong its front-page news value) would be rejected as too depressing. *Ace in the Hole* was possible in 1951 because films then cost less, more were made, and potential losses on a controversial picture would be cushioned by profits on many others.

Nevertheless, some out-of-the-ordinary films are still made today – generally because the distributor saw marketable qualities in the script that were unrealized or misunderstood. If a great deal of money has been spent on the picture, a dissatisfied distributor may ask the director to re-edit it or he may take it from him and cut it. If the picture cost little, it may simply be shelved or sold off to Home Box Office (an American pay-TV channel) for a song. The distributor has only one criterion: can his picture be shown universally with a fair chance of making a profit? If the answer is yes, massive amounts of money will swing behind the film to advertise and promote it. If the film seems to be of minority appeal, almost no money will be spent on promoting it even in those areas where it might do well. Why, after all, throw good money after bad? So the film fails commercially, which proves (doesn't it?) that they were right not to spend any more money on it.

This kind of circular reasoning has been the death knell of many an off-beat movie. Take Jonathan Demme's *Citizen's Band*. It is a human comedy based on character rather than action, with a picaresque narrative centred on the lore of CB radios. It is not a great film, but one of some charm, with potential appeal to the legion of American radio hams. They, however, never got to see it. The self-explanatory title was changed to the meaningless *Handle With Care* and the picture was dumped in out-of-the-way cinemas and flea-pits. *Citizen's Band* was never seen by its natural audience, though the film can still be caught from time to time on university campuses.

Commercial clout

That is more than can be said for an almost unknown picture that at least one respected critic (James Monaco) has hailed as a master-work. *Ganja & Hess* is a sophisticated vampire film made in 1973 by the black actor Bill Gunn, who had already written the script for Hal

Ashby's 1970 film *The Landlord*. To quote James Monaco:

> Almost before the credits have finished their cryptic roll in *Ganja &
> Hess*, you know you are watching an extraordinary film. Something
> about the voice of the film – its editing, camerawork, and point of
> view – tells you this experience will be unique. The film has a
> vitality that seems to broadcast itself. *American Film Now* (Oxford
> University Press)

But this heady brew of black fundamentalist Christianity, African
mythology, philosophy, drugs, sex and high living proved too much for
the distributor, the small, independent firm of Kelly-Jordan. It had
expected another black exploitation picture – *Blacula 1973*. Instead, it
had a close cousin to Georges Franju's *film maudit, Les Yeux Sans
Visage*.

Ganja & Hess opened with almost no publicity in New York and
closed after a week. Bill Gunn then took it to the Cannes film festival,
where it was shown out of competition several times and received a
standing ovation. Meanwhile, back home, Kelly-Jordan was strapped
for cash and disposed of *Ganja & Hess* to another company, Heritage
Enterprises. Ignorant of the film's success at Cannes, its new owners re-
edited the picture, added a different sound-track and additional scenes
not shot by Bill Gunn and sent it trundling around America under the
new title of *Blood Couple*. It is a travesty of *Ganja & Hess*.

The negative of the original film no longer exists. All that survives is
one print, held by the Museum of Modern Art in New York. It has
already been damaged in projection and is now withdrawn for its own
safety. Until a duplicate print can be made, one of the most
extraordinary and unorthodox films of the past ten years will remain
a legend.

Bill Gunn's film died not because of discrimination against a black
artist but because he had no commercial clout. More famous directors
who mystify their masters may at least be given first crack at making
over their work. It was Bernardo Bertolucci himself who took an hour
out of the original five-hour version of *1900*; Robert Altman dropped
several musical numbers from *Popeye* before it was widely released so
that it would not seem too long to children.

Length, indeed, is a prime constraint on film-makers. Two hours or
thereabouts is considered an ideal running time. It allows the exhibitor
to show the film five times a day. Three hours, too, is permissible: it
means fewer screenings, but tickets can be sold at enhanced prices.
Excessive, or in-between running times are regarded as commercially
difficult and there is likely to be strong pressure to cut the film down to

size. Sometimes this is done arbitrarily by distributors after the film has left its director.

Fifteen minutes were cut from Martin Scorsese's *New York, New York* in Britain to reduce it to 138 minutes; Stanley Kubrick's *The Shining* was pared from 146 to 119 minutes. Even worse affected was Robert Aldrich's *Twilight's Last Gleaming*. When first shown in Britain, the original 146-minute film was trimmed to 122 minutes. Sliced from the film was almost all the information that gave it political coherence, including a discussion of the supposed motives for America's involvement in the Vietnam war ('the objective of this war is to demonstrate to the Russians a brutal national will, that we have the willingness to inflict and suffer untold punishment. That no matter what the cost in American blood, we would perpetrate a theatrical holocaust').

The omission of dialogue like this could easily be interpreted as political censorship. Hollywood is no stranger to that. The vicious red-baiting of the House Un-American Activities Committee, subsequently taken up so aggressively by Senator Joseph McCarthy, drove many of the most talented men of the 1950s out of the American film industry. Abraham Polonsky was not able to direct a film for 20 years between *Force of Evil* (1949) and *Tell Them Willie Boy Is Here* (1969). Joseph Losey had to come to Britain and work for a time under an assumed name. In a different context, the American army suppressed John Huston's documentary *Let There Be Light* (about shell-shocked war veterans) for 34 years lest it deter recruits.

With *Twilight's Last Gleaming*, however, the truth is almost certainly nothing so sinister. The film, including the dialogue quoted above, was freely shown in America. It did extremely poorly at the box office, even though, beneath the politics, lay an exciting thriller about a nuclear hijacking, with the president of the United States held as hostage.

The British distributor, Hemdale, wanted a shorter and (as it hoped) more marketable picture emphasizing the action. In the event, audiences liked the shorter version no more than the longer one. So it was cut again and reissued three years later (in 1980) as *Nuclear Countdown*, running 92 minutes. By this point, some 54 minutes had gone from the original film, making the story virtually incomprehensible. But its 'sin' was never political; it just ran too long for an audience presumed to want only a diet of thick-eared melodrama.

Ironically, the most famous cinematic surgery job of modern times also took place on a picture with political overtones. Once again the patient seems to be dying. Michael Cimino's *Heaven's Gate* began as a western intended to cost $11.6m. United Artists backed it because its director had won considerable critical kudos and some box office success with his previous picture, *The Deer Hunter*.

Cimino saw the *Heaven's Gate* project as a grand statement about America, using the Johnson County range wars as a metaphor for the struggle between capitalism and socialism. Against this background, he intended to set a triangular love story in the hoary old tradition of *Gone With the Wind*. This, he thought, would commend it to United Artists. Cimino was a perfectionist. He spent and spent until everything was to his liking, in the process jacking up the budget from $11.6m to $35m and pushing out the running time to 219 minutes.

When *Heaven's Gate* was premiered in New York in November 1980, however, it received such negative reviews that Cimino himself begged United Artists to pull it back for further editing. At least, in this instance, Cimino was allowed to supervise the re-editing. He hacked 71 minutes out of his own film, sacrificing much of the beautiful photography that had been the one element admired in the original version. The revised picture re-surfaced in April to no kinder reviews and an even worse box office than before. Its fate is uncertain. What is certain is that, faced with a problem picture in future, the majors will be less inclined to allow its author second thoughts. They will want to re-cut it their way.

Personal pictures butchered

There is a long tradition of summary studio justice, beginning with Erich Von Stroheim's *Greed* in the 1920s and continuing through Huston's *The Red Badge of Courage* in the 1950s and Sam Peckinpah's *Major Dundee* in the 1960s to James Ivory's *The Wild Party* in the 1970s. All these films, though of unequal merit, were personal pictures, subsequently butchered by alien studio hands.

Few saw the first *Heaven's Gate* in the one week it played in New York, though letters published in the *New York Times* suggest that it was not, for all viewers, the unqualified disaster it was officially described by the critics. But to what kind of career can Cimino now look forward? What distributor will back him in future? A novelist or a playwright can take a wrong turning and swing back on course with his next work because the raw materials are so cheap. A film-maker cannot afford that luxury. In the old Hollywood adage, he is only as good as his last picture.

So what is to be done? Pauline Kael, the film critic of the *New Yorker*, has long advocated the establishment of a kind of film-makers' co-operative to challenge the entrenched power of the majors. United Artists itself, after all, was originally just such a venture. Experience suggests, however, that well-intentioned organizations of this kind are rapidly forced to adopt the same criteria as the majors in order to survive. In the early 1970s, Francis Coppola, Peter Bogdanovich and William Friedkin banded together to form the Directors Company within Paramount to handle their product. It failed to make its mark. So did First Artists, a similar company set up within Warner Bros. by the actors Paul Newman, Sidney Poitier and Barbra Streisand.

The low cost answer

The real answer lies in making the means of production less expensive. Motion pictures will never be as cheap as pen and paper, but they do not have to be as costly as a battleship. Thanks to inflation, the days of the one million dollar movie are gone for good, but technology exists for making pictures for substantially less than at present.

These techniques are being pioneered by Francis Coppola, himself an artist of some stature. His two *Godfather* films were both critical and commercial hits and *Apocalypse Now* was a blockbuster that did not insult the intelligence. With his personal earnings from these films, he has helped young film-makers to get started (e.g. Carroll Ballard, who made *The Black Stallion*); he persuaded Twentieth Century Fox to support Akira Kurosawa's *Kagemusha*; and he organized the American showings of the reconstituted silent classic, Abel Gance's *Napoleon*.

For all this, other artists owe him much. But his most exciting project is Zoetrope Studio, where his own new film, *One From the Heart*, has been made. Zoetrope is the ultimate high-technology studio, which makes use of video equipment and storyboarding techniques to reduce the time wastage that is one of the main components of the high cost of films. With this equipment, ideas can be tried out and rejected at an early, relatively cheap stage if they do not work. Theoretically, if it had been a Zoetrope production, the flaws in *Heaven's Gate* should have been identifiable, through preliminary rehearsals, long before $36m had been spent.

The equipment used at Zoetrope becomes progressively more economic with every film made there. Initially, however, it was expensive to install and all the costs had to be borne by the first film – *One From the Heart*. It was thanks only to a $1m bridging loan from Paramount and a subsequent cash injection from the millionaire Jack Singer that Coppola was able to keep his head above water. But that crisis seems now to be over, which should mean that the facilities at Zoetrope will be available in future for other experimental films.

Politics and Porn: How France Defends Society and Human Dignity

Martyn Auty

Evidence of film censorship in France has tended to surface sporadically during the last fifty years, almost always at times of national crisis – World War I, the *Front Populaire* in the mid-thirties, the German occupation, the Algerian war, May 1968, and so on. It is important to emphasize two modes of film censorship: the first, self-evident state intervention in the process of cinema either at the point of production, distribution or exhibition; the second, 'invisible', ideologically conditioned, leading to self-censorship.

The history of film censorship in France during World War II is a complex skein of suppression and betrayal that resulted in the silencing or enforced emigration of certain key film-makers and charges of collaboration against those who continued to work under the Vichy government. To combat the rigid regulations of the Nazi-supervised French film censors, some writers and directors opted for the use of historical allegory, e.g. Marcel Carné's *Les Visiteurs du Soir* ('Night Visitors') as a form of subversive cinema.

Under the Fifth Republic, the structure for maintaining a tight rein on the cinema altered little from that instituted during the occupation, and with the escalation of the Algerian war, control of the cinema was consolidated by civil servants who staffed the short chain of command that connected the French Censorship Board with the Ministry of Information. Jean-Luc Godard's *Le Petit Soldat* ('The Little Soldier') (1960) was the most celebrated victim of direct censorship, but several other films that similarly sought to expose the French army's brutality and torture in Algeria were also banned in the period 1959–62.

At that time the director Claude Autant-Lara (who had seen his

Vol. 10, no. 4, 1981

1947 film *Le Diable au Corps* ('The Devil in Him') subjected to censorship of a peculiarly nationalist and even racist nature) found that the original title *L'Objecteur* ('The Objector') for his 1961 film (about a conscientious objector) had to be changed to *Tu Ne Tueras Point* ('You Shall Not Kill') before the censors would grant the film a 'visa de contrôle'. The film was released at a critical moment in the Algerian war when more and more Frenchmen were either deserting or refusing to be drafted.

In February 1968 the government suspicious of the radical film-makers and students who frequented the Cinémathèque Française, fired its director, Henri Langlois, and provoked a near-riot which was one of the first mass public demonstrations to anticipate the events of May 1968 in Paris.

Under Pompidou's presidency the Commission de Contrôle Cinématographique (the official film censorship body) perpetuated the notion of a division between 'subversive' and 'pornographic' material, insisting that these were quite distinct categories to be assessed according to separate criteria. Films like Andy Warhol and Paul Morrissey's *Trash* tested this argument with their subversive combinations of sex, drugs and an alternative society. The pigeon-holing of censorable subjects was gradually exposed as a fabrication.

It couldn't happen here

Another test case of 1972 teased out the political stance of the Commission de Contrôle. An Italian film by Damiano Damiani dealing with corruption and rioting in a Rome prison was to have been released in France under the title *Nous Sommes Tous en Liberté Provisoire* ('We Are All in Provisional Freedom'). When the French censors saw the film they demanded cuts which the distributors felt would emasculate the film. In defiance, the distributor decided to release the film intact under a direct translation of its Italian title: *L'Instruction Préliminaire est Close: Oubliez-la* ('The Preliminary Enquiry is Secret: Forget It'). Once again the censors objected. Undaunted, the distributor called a press conference, gave a sneak preview of the film, and won the support of a powerful lobby of journalists who then campaigned for the film's release, uncut. The Commission de Contrôle climbed down but insisted on a warning to be placed in the foyer of all cinemas where the film was shown to the effect that this was an Italian film and that it depicted events (notably prison riots) which could obviously not happen here ...

In the early seventies state intervention in cinema took an even more curious turn with the delayed release of the Ken Loach-Tony

Garnett film *Family Life*. On this occasion too a prominent warning was required by the Commission de Contrôle to the effect that the film showed a teenage girl in the course of a serious mental illness and as such might be found disturbing. Clearly the censors themselves had found the film a disturbing experience – as they should – and its subversive force was obviously not lost on them. But their intervention, which is an ironic parallel to the meddlesome and harmful intervention of the doctors and parents in the film, raises the spectre of political censorship again.

No more censorship?

On his election in 1974, President Giscard d'Estaing announced that there would be no more censorship in France. But, countered some sceptics, there had been no official censorship for years (at least not called censorship), so why suddenly announce an end to censorship?

It was not long before the suspicions aroused by Giscard's declaration found a basis in fact. The Commission de Contrôle was to gain assistance from the new right-wing government in its task of 'cleaning up' the cinema and stemming the tide of pornographic films. At the same time, the new President took a long hard look at the French TV network and, in the name of free enterprise, broke up the existing ORTF into smaller 'more competitive' units. This enabled Giscard to introduce new laws regulating the cinema and to construct a new chain of command in television that gave him unprecedented power over what was said and shown on French TV. In essence Giscard's policy was to subdue the large screen while gaining greater control over the small. The record of his exercise of power within the television structure and his far-reaching powers of censorship is another story, but it should be borne in mind, especially in the light of the close collaboration between the film and TV industries in France, where movies are often co-produced with television and therefore subject to the same frame of reference as other TV material.

Thus in 1975 a bill, presented by Jean Foyer, was debated in the French National Assembly. This bill sought the suppression of films that attacked human dignity and incited violation of fundamental rights; and of publicity material related to pornographic films or films devoted to crime or violence. A strong Catholic lobby backed these proposals and sections of the women's movement also offered qualified support. French films that were judged pornographic would cease to be eligible for state aid under the new law and producers pre-selling such films could be liable to heavy (retroactive) fines were their film to be judged pornographic once completed.

Two features of crucial importance emerged from this debate. First, by placing the emphasis on pornography, the government turned the spotlight away from the question of 'touchy' political subjects which documentarists were having trouble making, and they legitimized their crack-down on censorship in the eyes of many politicians previously opposed to film censorship; second, the use of economic sanctions would encourage self-censorship.

The President of the Commission de Contrôle in 1975 spoke of a subtle interchange between film company administrators and film producers who agree 'in advance' on certain cuts because they feel that otherwise their films would encounter problems obtaining the visa. From the point of view of the Commission, the more give and take that went on among film production companies the easier their task, both practically and ideologically.

Just before he died, the Paris Cinémathèque director Henri Langlois praised the American TV series *Washington Behind Closed Doors* for its attack on American institutions. 'Could you image anyone wanting to make *Elysée Behind Closed Doors*? He wouldn't be able to shoot two metres.' As an anonymous critic put it in April 1981, 'Anyone wanting to make a film about the Bokassa diamonds is going to have a hard time. I happen to know two people who began working on a documentary about the affair but stopped after they received death threats.'

Answering the charge of state inviolability, the Commission de Contrôle points to the existence of legislation intended to protect the dignity of the head of state and insists that cinema, as much as literature and the press, is subject to this legislation. By extension, all the major institutions are thus protected from discredit. The French navy, for example, provided problems for director Christian Jacque when a member of the Commission objected to a scene where a monkey was dressed as a naval rating in his comedy *Premier Bal* ('First Ball'). A Japanese film, whose French title was to have been *L'Aubergine est Farcie* ('The Stuffed Aubergine'), was refused importation on the grounds of its adverse depiction of the police. Another film banned in the mid-seventies was an American documentary called *Skezag* which dealt with drug addiction among Vietnam veterans.

Certain *causes célèbres* from French history prove the point. The first film to be made about the Dreyfus affair was in 1899 – it was also the last on the subject until a telefilm a couple of years ago. By then the official but unwritten taboo had been broken. Stanley Kubrick's acclaimed anti-war film *Paths of Glory* (1957), dealing with a French general who massacres his own troops in an ill-judged action during

World War I, was banned from French screens until 1977. That same year *La Question* ('The Question'), showing the torture used by French troops in Algeria, met with considerable delays from the Commission de Contrôle, delays that the director Laurent Heynemann saw as contributing to the release of his picture in high summer, the worst time of the year to open a film in France. An earlier film, *Dehors Dedans* ('Outside Inside') by Alain Fleischer, was an even more flagrant example of the delay tactic. Here the film was recalled for a second viewing by the Commission on the day it was due to be press-shown and only days before its intended release. For a low-budget film such an action is disastrous, since without publicity and reviews box-office failure is almost certain.

The case of *Dehors Dedans* followed immediately in the wake of the Foyer legislation which introduced the procedure of banning certain films to people under 18 and taxing such films at 33 per cent (instead of the normal 17 per cent). Any film banned to under-eighteens was taxable at these rates under the law of 1975, so films by Bergman, Losey, Pasolini, Fellini and many other world-acclaimed cineastes suffered financially alongside home-grown French films which had sexuality and violence as themes in the argument of the work.

Violence, porn and politics

During October–November 1975 – the high-point of the debate – film-makers, producers, film trade-unionists, critics and teachers all protested against Jean Foyer's legislation. Beneath the 'anti-porn' campaign they saw a concerted attempt to bridle and silence French cinema. What may have seemed to some a paranoid reaction was, however, proved correct when the next few years revealed the extent of censorship that had gone on in the business of purchasing cinema films for transmission on television. A glance down the list of those rejected (for example Yannick Bellon's exemplary anti-rape film *L'Amour Violé* – 'too disturbing') testified to the authorities' interest in discouraging contentious material.

'Never before,' declared the text of the trade unionists' protest, 'has censorship in France gone so far. Never have the public and the intellectuals been held in such contempt. Never has freedom of expression been so threatened.' After 1000 people demonstrated on the Champs Elysées, the Foyer bill was modified to the effect that among those films banned to the under-eighteens, only 'pornographic' films would be liable for the 50 per cent salary deductions levied on this category of films. By mid-1976 the situation was clarified to the extent that films in the 'sex and violence' category entailed a double levy of TVA (comparable to VAT in the UK) for any cinema playing them, and producers of such films would lose any possibility of state aid for a year.

Even those critics who accepted the necessity for a measure of censorship on pornographic films, posed the crucial question of how the Commission (25 people drawn from the civil service, education, clinical psychiatry and the film business) was to decide what was and was not 'pornographic'. Films such as *Last Tango in Paris* would pose problems directly analogous to the publications of Baudelaire's *Les Fleurs du Mal* or Flaubert's *Madame Bovary*. Besides it was – and still is – argued by some that pornography is a sexually and therefore politically liberating experience. Followers of Reich might aver that pornography carried a revolutionary charge, an idea that underpins the Yugoslav film *Sweet Movie* banned in certain parts of France but still shown in some towns. Among those favouring censorship of pornographic films are many Socialist deputies who speak of it as being 'a dangerous evolution in society' and 'threatening to bring about the bankruptcy of French cinema'.

Ranged against such arguments are those who see the repression of pornography as a politically repressive move and who contest the claim that porno-films have hastened the decline of smaller cinemas in non-metropolitan areas. In the smaller towns it has been statistically established that the film trade was dying slowly before 'middle-class' porn (e.g. *Emanuelle*) revived business in the mid-seventies.

Few intelligent observers, however, can have been blind to the fact that 'the defence of human dignity' was an objective used by the Giscard government to 'outlaw' pornographic films and as a pretext to introduce legislation that would control the cinema in general. The film director Michel Drach recently commented, 'There is censorship, and it is the worst kind – economic censorship. For example, if *Last Tango* did not carry Brando's name and Bertolucci's reputation it would straightaway be taxed as pornographic.'

In the second half of Giscard's presidency the issue of censorship continued to focus on the arguments surrounding pornography. On the right wing, Jacques Marette of the UDF (Giscard's party) claims, 'Pornography poses the problem of the defence of our society'. For the left, the journalist Jean-Louis Bory says, 'By this legislation the liberal society of Giscard d'Estaing drops its mask and proves that its celebrated liberalism is a token liberalism. By this law, proposed and passed by irresponsible illiterates, censorship was re-established – it has killed what was freest and most innovative in the cinema. The "invasion of pornography", regrettable in itself, only served as a pretext.' That the contemporary French cinema has rarely looked and sounded so complacent may be at least partially attributable to the fact that selfcensorship has done its job and in this way the institutions of Giscard's France have escaped genuine criticism on the screen. It remains to be seen if Mitterrand's presidency can set about dismantling the apparatus of censorship.

Britain: Out of Fear and Ignorance

Guy Phelps

'Film, in our view, is a uniquely powerful instrument; the close-up, fast cutting, the sophistication of modern make-up and special effects techniques, the heightening effect of sound effects and music, all combine on the large screen to produce an effect which no other medium can create.' With these words the Williams Report on Obscenity and Film Censorship of November 1979 not only lost control of its literary style but also abruptly abandoned its principle of liberalization of censorship (the printed word was recommended to be freed of all restriction) to put forward what *The Times* called 'an apparatus of censorship exceeding in severity anything known at present to the laws of England'.

It is easy to pour scorn on this apparent paradox, but Professor Williams and his committee did not reach their conclusions without due thought and without presenting a lengthy defence of their recommendations. All of which goes to prove that censorship is a complex topic where fact and theory, law and morality, art and science meet headlong in a thicket of confusion. Anyone seeking to construct a liberal censorship has to confront the inherent contradiction in terms.

The present British system is a unique and illogical compromise arrived at in a totally haphazard fashion – a historical accident. The Cinematograph Act of 1909 was passed by Parliament 'simply to secure safety in the construction of buildings in which inflammable films are exhibited'. Thus cinemas were brought within the licensing arrangements of local authorities in the same way as theatres, music halls, etc. The Act, however, allowed councils to impose whatever conditions they wished 'so long as those conditions are not unreasonable'. Against all expectation and intention, the courts ruled that it was not unreasonable to include specifications as to film content.

Already of course the cinema had been blamed for almost every social calamity of the preceding decade with the possible exception of the Boer War. Clergymen, police chiefs and right-thinking people everywhere inveighed against this venal form of entertainment which was available to the poor and illiterate.

A horrified industry reacted by appointing its own 'official' censor, and the British Board of Film Censors (BBFC) started work in 1913. As a purely advisory body the Board was widely ignored by local authorities, naturally suspicious of its avowed 'independence'. So much so that in 1916 the Home Office announced the imminent establishment of a government-appointed censorship body. But Prime Minister Asquith fell and the scheme was dropped.

When in 1920 the influential London and Middlesex County Councils adopted the BBFC's certificates as requirement for their licences, the tide turned. Within a short time the Board was established as the basis for the censorship system, its decisions almost universally accepted by the statutory censors, the local authorities.

Although set up by the film industry, the Board was designed to be 'a purely independent and impartial body' and its independence from the trade was, from the first, quite genuine. Independence of government, on the other hand, was another matter. Eager to establish itself, the Board acquiesced in accepting whatever lead the government might give and even actively sought guidance on controversial matters. Both bodies were part of an establishment existing to protect a public that was assumed to include 'a not inconsiderable proportion of people of immature judgment'. Consequently, as John Trevelyan, Secretary of the BBFC from 1957 to 1971 has commented, 'up to the last war the Board clearly considered itself the guardian of public morality, allowing no departure from the accepted code of conduct and behaviour, the protector of the establishment, the protector of the reputation and image of Britain in other countries, and the protector of cinema audiences from such dangerous themes as those involving controversial politics'. Not surprisingly, many films fell foul of this overtly paternalistic and political censorship, Eisenstein (of course) and D. W. Griffith (more surprisingly) being among the many to have works proscribed.

Changing times

Since 1945 the Board has been steadily liberalized. In 1951 the 'X' certificate (limiting audiences to those aged 16 and over) was introduced in addition to the purely advisory 'U' and 'A' with which all films had had hitherto to conform (apart from the period of the short-lived 'H' – for Horror – certificate). But even in the fifties certain attitudes and opinions were rigorously suppressed. In 1955 *Rebel Without a Cause* was pruned of scenes of anti-social or rebellious behaviour, particularly where they reflected discredit on the hero's parents. It was evidently not thought acceptable to suggest that adults might be in any way responsible for the unhappiness and waywardness of their children.

But times were changing fast. The passing of the Obscene Publications Act in 1959 (which applies only to England and Wales) – even though it specifically excluded films – marked a major breakthrough. Its acceptance that publication of an obscene article could be justified if it were 'for the public good on the grounds that it is in the interest of science, literature, art or learning, or of other objects of general concern' enabled the Board to make similar allowances for films. During the sixties commercial cinema clubs appeared, offering a limited outlet for films not certificated by the Board, while by 1970 the range of films passed called for a further review of the classification with cut-offs at age 14 ('AA') and 18 ('X').

The early seventies saw a major collision between opposing points of view. The backlash against the liberalization of the fifties and early sixties in many areas related to sex, reached a climax with the emergence of bodies like the Festival of Light and individuals like Lord Longford and Mary Whitehouse.

The film industry, forced to concentrate on 'adult' material by the stranglehold on the family audience now held by television, proved to be the battleground. The BBFC found itself caught in the crossfire. A series of court cases offered conclusive proof that legal action was an unsatisfactory system for handling censorship, and hastened the extension of the Obscene Publications Act to cover the cinema in 1977. In future prosecution of film producers or distributors could only take place with the consent of the Director of Public Prosecutions. In addition, the test of criminality became not merely offensiveness but actual harm to the morality of a significant proportion of the likely audience.

This change was heartily supported by the BBFC whose current Secretary, James Ferman, argues that it has made a real difference in the approach that the Board can adopt. Not only does the Act insist that films be judged as a whole with less attention paid to individual specific ingredients, but the test of 'deprave and corrupt' which the Act applies allows a distinction to be drawn between manners and morals, obscenity and mere indecency. The latter is an issue of manners no longer subject to judicial control which is confined to obscenity, an issue of morals.

But the Board is not simply an interpreter of the law. While films must be examined in the light of the various statutes – the Cinematograph (Animals) Act of 1937 and the Protection of Children Act of 1978 which regulate the use of animals and children under 16 during filing must also be considered – the Board must ensure that films are likely to be acceptable to the 330 licensing authorities; or perhaps, to be more accurate, that its general policy is acceptable to local councils. In this it has been largely successful. Since the years of confrontation over *The Devils*, *A Clockwork Orange*, *Last Tango in Paris* and others local activity has rarely reached a level to be worthy of wide media coverage. Today perhaps 70 councils take some regular interest in censorship, despite the fact that the Board is now vastly less restrictive than previously and adopts a policy that is probably more liberal than any Council: the supply of local certificates granted to films rejected by the Board has virtually dried up. Table 1 indicates the changes of the last few years. Clearly the number of films cut has declined greatly, even among those given 'X' certificates, and fewer films are now rejected, although this statistic should be treated with caution: only films likely to be acceptable are shown to the Board.

Table 1. Films cut and rejected 1974–80

Year	Total	'U'	'A'	'AA'	'X'	Rejected
1974	540 (218)	72 (5)	80 (23)	93 (21)	268 (169)	27
1976	402 (135)	53 (3)	73 (17)	74 (10)	187 (105)	15
1978	324 (74)	35 (2)	81 (16)	66 (8)	138 (48)	4
1980	319 (67)	24 (0)	82 (9)	84 (4)	124 (54)	4

Number of films cut given in parentheses.

Rare controversy

The Board's scissors (purely figurative: all cutting is actually done by the distributor or producer involved) are now generally reserved for violence, particularly in a sexual context. 'There is evidence,' Ferman has written, 'that the combination of sex and violence may have an unhealthy influence on some members of an audience, and the Board has always exercised control over such material even where it is not covered by the criminal law.' There is, of course, no *conclusive* evidence, but the Board's caution is understandable in an area of few certainties. Where 'extreme' violence is involved the Board prefers to pass responsibility to the statutory bodies – implying that councillors, answerable to the public at the polls, are the appropriate ones to make such decisions.

Except that film censorship is never an election issue, and to confuse such decisions with local party politics and all the other considerations of local government, seems unsatisfactory. Many councils themselves – not to mention the Association of Metropolitan Authorities – do not see this as a proper function of local government, and there is little doubt that councillors generally are ill-equipped to plunge into these unfamiliar and murky depths. One of the rare controversies is instructive on this point. *Monty Python's Life of Brian* attracted some criticism on account of its supposed blasphemy. Widespread media coverage encourage 101 councils to view the film. Of these, 62 simply confirmed the Board's 'AA' certificate. But 28 enforced a local 'X' and 11 banned the film altogether. Ironically, the Board discovered that 'the final decision was rarely determined by the issue of blasphemy'.

Weighing up a great deal of evidence presented to them, the Williams Committee unhesitatingly proposed that local authorities should have their powers removed. More contentiously, the Committee also called for the abolition of the BBFC and its replacement by a statutory body with the formal powers currently vested in local government. Closer examination reveals that what they suggest is not so different from the BBFC after all. They propose two levels within the operation. The lower tier doing the day-to-day work is merely the present secretary and examiners of the BBFC under another guise. The upper tier would be a broadly-based body to hear appeals against decisions. This function is currently fulfilled by the President of the BBFC, so all that is really envisaged is replacement of the President by a Committee. The change is more apparent than real.

Dangers of state control

The true innovation, of course, would be that the new body would be 'official' with all the inherent dangers of state-controlled censorship. Doubts as to how far these dangers had been really considered by the Committee were strengthened when, within a few months, David Robinson, the one Committee member with real knowledge of film, admitted that the establishment of a statutory Examining Board would be 'a determined move towards a formal and official censorship which at present does not exist ... would reintroduce government censorship in this country, with all that might imply'. Yet the Committee advocated such a move without offering any substantial criticism of the present set-up, or indeed without being aware of any 'proof' that censorship is necessary in the first place – other than that it is widely felt that 'caution' is wise in view of the power of the film medium and the doubts held about its 'effects' on audiences.

Evidently the Committee, which had been established by the Labour government to investigate the whole area of obscenity and film censorship, was jolted out of its basic liberalism by revulsion at the sadism, bestiality and extreme violence exhibited in banned films they were shown during their enquiry. Such movies are regularly produced in certain countries and few would advocate their open availability here. The need to protect children, and the need to proscribe exhortations to racial hatred and violence, are widely accepted. In which case, one is concerned simply with where and by whom the line is to be drawn. The Williams Committee's suggestions present many problems – their blueprint would probably be unworkable.

It is a fact that, under the present arrangements, few important films have been completely banned in recent years. Oshima's highly explicit *Empire of the Senses* could never be considered likely to satisfy local authorities, but it has been quite widely exhibited under club conditions. Anyone who really wanted to see it could certainly have done so. Pasolini's *Salo* is a rare example of an arguably important picture that has been restricted. This film, an up-dating of de Sade's *120 Days of Sodom* to a World War Two setting, was described by Ferman as 'one of the most disturbing ever to be seen by the Board, yet its purpose is deeply serious ... it is quite certainly shocking, disgusting and revolting – even in the legal sense – but it is meant to be. He (Pasolini) wants us to be appalled at the atrocities of which human nature is capable when absolute power is wielded corruptly'.

The Director of Public Prosecutions indicated that anyone showing the complete version would be prosecuted, and a cut version was achieved only with difficulty, the censor fearing that 'cuts would destroy the film's purpose by making the horrors less revolting, and therefore more acceptable'.

Castrating *Caligula*

The most recent subject of 'concern' has been the film *Caligula*. This production started life as a screenplay by the distinguished American writer Gore Vidal, based on Suetonius' *Lives of the Twelve Caesars*. Finance for 'Gore Vidal's Caligula' was provided by *Penthouse* magazine, whose chief, Bob Guccione, engaged as director Tinto Brass, best known for his Nazi-sex film *Salon Kitty*. Brass' interpretation of Vidal's screenplay was not quite what the writer had in mind and he was forced to ask that his name be entirely removed from the film. However, Brass' version also failed to satisfy Guccione, for rather different reasons. Guccione had set his heart (and wallet) on making the ultimate sex-epic, on a budget never before allotted to such a project and with all the (historically quite accurate) horrors and varied sexual activity portrayed in glorious close-up. He himself filmed additional episodes which can accurately be described as 'hard-core' pornography. At which point Brass too cried 'Enough' and his only credit on the finished film is as cinematographer.

Guccione's inserts guaranteed massive publicity for 'the most controversial film of the eighties'. Vitriolic reviews and huge audiences were the inevitable result. In Britain a six-month struggle to achieve a showable version ensued. The Customs Act of 1876 required the removal of much explicitly sexual footage, and the Obscene Publications Act took care of some violent – and particularly sexually violent – material. This was sufficient to allow exhibition in unlicensed clubs, but for public exhibition a further three minutes had to be removed to satisfy local authorities that their populaces were not likely to be outrageously offended. With some ten minutes gone, the film was presumably returned to something like Tinto Brass' version, with Guccione's improvements consigned to the cutting-room floor.

The Board was, naturally, criticized for castrating *Caligula*, but the question obviously arises as to what is the authentic version. One could well argue that *Caligula* had been treated to sexual athletics and violence for which he had never been originally intended. As so often happens, the final print of this film bears only a tenuous relationship to the original intentions of the 'creative' participants. Guccione, like many producers before him, has exercised his option, as financer, to ensure that *his* version survives. The fact is that money not only talks: it pays the piper and can impose the tune. Censors, official or unofficial, can only modulate the occasional note. For every film banned to the sound of righteous condemnation, a thousand are silently lost, never made because their ideas were not considered attractive and potentially lucrative by the very small body of men who control the pursestrings of the industry.

The tiny selection of scripts that do attract investment and become films are in the process subject to constant supervision, control and outright censorship. The film-makers are creating a 'product' that will have to be sold, and sold very widely, if the vast sums that films cost nowadays are to be recouped. The concept of freedom of expression is not one that carries much weight in this most ruthless and practical of worlds.

Tight grip

To be seen by a substantial audience a film must be distributed by one of the handful of companies which dominate the circulation of films in this country. The major companies fall into two categories. On the one hand are Rank, EMI and ACC. These three British companies also control the three largest exhibition circuits (Odeon, ABC and Classic). Until Rank withdrew from production last year, all three were involved at that stage also. All three have major interests in television (Southern, Thames and ATV), and two of them own record companies. In all three cases only a small proportion of turnover is accounted for by film – perhaps 15 per cent in the case of Rank, 20 per cent at ACC and as little as 5 per cent at EMI (now part of the Thorn empire).

The other major distributors are the British offices of the American companies – Fox, United Artists, Columbia, Warner Bros, Paramount, MGM and Universal. In Britain these companies have been 'rationalized' into larger groupings so that the effective outlets are even fewer. Of these seven, five are subsidiaries of conglomerates.

They are also the main production companies, so that their grip on the film industry is tight. As cogs in the big business wheel the purpose of the studios now is not to make films, but to make money. The studio executives decide what is to be made and seen in America and Britain and their decisions are made in the context of their roles in the big conglomerate world. Not surprisingly the range of ideas that survives the tortuous process of successfully seeking financial backing is not remarkably wide.

And not all films made are ever seen. At the exhibition stage, the control is even tighter. The programming of the two main circuits, which between them own about one-third of all screens (including most of the big and lucrative ones) rests in the hands of two men. Rejection by them condemns a film to a much reduced audience through the smaller circuit and independent cinemas. A Monopolies Commission is presently studying the situation, but its findings and subsequent action – if any – will be too late to prevent the massively destructive effect that this duopoly has had on the cinema in this country.

Some near-misses of recent months indicate the sort of censorship that this system is capable of inflicting. Polanski's *Tess*, a Franco-British co-production, was rejected by every distribution company and seemed likely never to be seen here, despite its origins in Hardy's very English novel. Only the huge commercial success of the film in America finally pushed Columbia into a change of mind. Scorses's *Raging Bull* was rejected by the Rank circuit on the gut-reaction of its booker, and it was only the retirement of this gentleman that enabled the film to get the sort of treatment it deserved.

The script for Richard Rush's *Stuntman* was rejected by every studio; independently financed after seven years' struggle the finished film was then turned down by every distributor. Rush opened the film in Seattle, without a distributor, and broke all the house records. Finally distributed by Fox, it won Festival prizes and was a commercial success.

Stuntman was eventually nominated for two Oscars – Best Direction and Best Actor (Peter O'Toole). *Tess* and *Raging Bull* were both films which won several Oscars. Thus three of the six films nominated for the two top Academy Awards in 1981 encountered difficulties in reaching our screens. It needs little imagination to realize that many 'smaller' (or less fortunate) films sink out of sight under such a system.

As a result, even American films have only a small chance of being widely seen. Films from elsewhere fare considerably worse. Each year about 4000 films are made around the world: only 300–350 are ever seen in Britain. The fact that America makes only some 5 per cent of the world's pictures would be hard to guess from a British viewpoint. India, Japan, Turkey, Italy and France all make more, but the trickle of films from such countries reaching our screens is indicative of the sort of selection procedures that put the activities of local councillors and even the Board of Censors into pretty grim perspective.

For the 'censors' themselves are simply the last in a long line of people who can alter a film after the director has submitted his version. At many stages in the transition from first cut to exhibition in a cinema a film may be cut or, to all intents and purposes, banned from public view by people merely making the commercial decisions for which they are paid. There are aspects of the system, however, which it is less easy to accept, notably the monolithic structure of the industry in this country, particularly at the exhibition stage, which imposes a highly restrictive censorship, one result of which has been the virtual disappearance of British film production. The present study being undertaken by the Monopolies Commission offers far greater possibilities for freedom for film-makers and audiences in this country than any analysis of the censorship system itself could suggest.

Eastern Europe: Thaws, Booms and Blacklists

A. J. Liehm

There is no doubt that the nationalized film industries of the USSR and of Eastern Europe have made an important contribution to the development of film art. The Soviet avant-garde, Eisenstein, Kuleshov, Pudovkin, Dovzhenko, Vertov, Kozinstev, and many others, spring readily to mind. But there was also the world's first nationalized film industry in Budapest during the short-lived Hungarian Soviet republic in 1919 which – under the leadership of a young, ardent revolutionary called Sándor Korda (Sir Alexander Korda in later years) – embarked on the most ambitious project ever, filming the 100 great classics of world literature. Korda's aim was to develop the language of film, enhance the cultural prestige of the new art, and bring these works to the masses (not exactly the same ideas which inspired Lenin's words about film being 'the most important art for us'). Even the Soviet output of the 1930s cannot be entirely dismissed; some French and Italian directors have studied the best films of that time very closely, not to mention Laurence Olivier's detailed study of Eisenstein's only socialist-realist picture, *Alexander Nevsky*.

After World War II there were first the Hungarians again (1953–6) with their own version of the new style introduced to world cinema by Italian neo-realism, the first original influence of post-war East European cinema, felt mostly in the other countries of Eastern Europe. Then came the Polish school, the romantic 'Polishness' of Andrzej Wajda (with an added touch of expressionism in his early films), the biting ironies of Munk, the psychological dramas of Kawalerowicz. The two schools, however, did not survive the 'normalization' which followed the revolts of 1956. While the Hungarian revival was crushed immediately and died in the ashes of

Budapest, the Polish one was progressively strangled. After the tragic death of Munk, only Wajda was left to wage his lonely battle.

In the Soviet Union, the promising rebirth of the Soviet cinema which started almost immediately after Stalin's death in 1953, continued with all its ups and downs through the uncertainties of the Khrushchev period and even – in a way – until 1968, when, in the aftermath of the invasion of Czechoslovakia, a cultural policy was finally established.

The longest spell of relative freedom was the one experienced in Czechoslovakia between 1961 and 1968 (after a promising but short-lived interlude in 1955–8). It produced what was called 'the Czechoslovak Film Miracle' creating, mostly in the work of the youngest directors, a new style which was to influence film-making throughout the world.

In the mid-sixties the Hungarians, too, made a comeback. In the last 15 years they have not only produced one of the most important figures of contemporary world cinema, Miklós Jancsó, but also an uninterrupted flow of high quality films, some of them astonishingly open in assessing the recent past, yet with their eye always on the present.

Yugoslavia experienced its most interesting artistic film boom in the second half of the 1960s, when the 'new film' movement coincided with the removal of Rankovich – the powerful head of the secret police – and the so-called 'second revolution'. Its end came together with the crushing of the Croatian national revival in the early seventies and the general anti-intellectual campaign which accompanied it. Two of the most outstanding Yugoslav film-makers, Dusan Makavejev and Alexander Petrovich, left the country to work abroad, thus joining not only the Poles (Polanski and Skolimowski), but also a large bunch of gifted Czechs – Passer, Forman, Jasný, Nemec, the late Jan Kadar, and many others – whose emigration, however, was to become permanent. They again were soon joined by Soviet Jewish émigré film-makers of talent such as Bogin, Gabay, Kalik, etc.

The fortunes of the Bulgarian cinema can be summed up briefly: having built a film industry after World War II and acquired all the necessary skills, the Bulgarians repeatedly surprised the world as extremely gifted and original film-makers. Unfortunately, the careers of the leading directors have, for three generations now, been interrupted, again and again, the cultural thaws invariably being short-lived exceptions rather than attempts at a defined policy. Thus, none of the promising artists had time to create a consistent *oeuvre*.

In Rumania, the spells of free cinematic expression were still more short-lived and fortuitous. Nevertheless, in his *Reconstruction*, the theatre director Lucian Pintillie created one of the best and most profound East European films ever, which unfortunately was also his last. He has since been working in the theatre abroad, as has his colleague, Liviu Ciulei. Another extraordinary talent among the Rumanians, Radu Gabrea, simply left for the West and gave up making films.

While in Czechoslovakia the seventies were a dark period, with almost no films of interest being made (the only, qualified, exception being the two recent pictures by Vera Chytilová) and no new talent of importance emerging, Poland experienced a most astonishing revival. Beginning in 1970, prior to the first revolt in the northern ports, it continued despite serious obstacles, throughout the seventies until it established itself, at the end of the decade and at the very beginning of the eighties, as an emerging great power not only of East European but of European cinema as a whole. The veteran of the early battles of the 1950s was Andrzej Wajda, joined some time ago by Krzystof Zanussi, and the two today belong to the most important film-makers in the world. In their wake comes a large number of new names, whose talents should be able to mature fully in the 1980s.

The state as producer

As in all other fields of artistic expression, censorship has many faces. One could say that – with the exception of open dictatorships (usually in countries where film production does not play an important role) – post-production censorship by boards – on political or moral grounds – has been replaced by surveillance by the producer, by the distributor, by different groups representing the market. Such censorship, with its special forms in TV, can be – and usually is – as, if not more, efficient than censorship by a committee. Nowadays these forms prevail also in the countries of the Soviet bloc.

This explains, on the one hand, why it is not easy to compile lists of censored films, those shelved being the exception rather than the rule. On the other hand, it also explains why in almost all countries of the area (the GDR and Rumania perhaps being the only exceptions, but even these with certain qualifications) there have been periods of extreme, almost free, blossoming of the cinema; why great film-makers have emerged there, creating *oeuvres* of international significance; and why films openly critical of these countries' shortcomings, problems, and even their very political system have been produced and distributed abroad by their state-owned and state-supervised film industries.

The reasons are relatively simple. The publicly owned and heavily subsidized film industry is a prestigious undertaking which originated in Lenin's famous and sometimes misunderstood utterance about 'film as the most important art'. Unlike the Hungarians in 1919, what Lenin really had in mind was what TV has become – a powerful mass communication medium to be used for the purposes of propaganda and education. However, even if these aims are always present in the minds of those who own and run the nationalized film industries, another idea – that of subsidized cinematic art, liberated from the dictates of the market and making use of the advantages enjoyed by subsidized theatre, music, art galleries, museums, public buying and so on – has never been lost.

A subsidized film industry naturally presents enormous advantages for film production and the development of film art, which is to a large extent liberated from the pressures of the market and the lowest levels of taste and understanding: the situation here is in a way similar to that publicly supported TV. There is, of course, a price to be paid in the existence of a single, excessively powerful producer – the state. As long as this state – in our case a Communist one – knows exactly what it wants and what it doesn't, as long as there is a more or less unanimous consensus on the part of the powers that be, all the benefits the cinema could obtain from its nationalized structure are, so to speak, suspended (although the degree of this suspension varies). On the other hand, whenever the state, the 'establishment', does not know exactly where it stands, what is going to happen tomorrow, that is in moments of political, economic and social crisis and periods of uncertainty, all the advantages of a subsidized film production begin to function (again in various degrees and for different periods), the film-makers are in charge, and their art flourishes to an astonishing extent.

As the production of a feature film usually takes a year or more, and because the periods mentioned above are of uncertain duration, a conflict typical of the situation in a nationalized film industry occurs. Films which originated in one situation may be completed under totally different circumstances, with different political guidelines in force and often with different people in charge. It is at times such as these that the administrative censorship takes charge, that films are shelved, their makers black-listed, projects discontinued . . . .

Forbidden films

Let us consider some actual examples. The first nationalized film industry to react against the Stalinist political (but mostly aesthetic) dogmas was the Hungarian. In the period between 1953 and 1956, films were produced which, while not attacking the system politically, represented an artistic departure from the sterile propagandistic academicism of the preceding period, replacing it with a lively representation of everyday life, drawing its inspiration chiefly from Italian neo-realism. When the Hungarian revolution was crushed in November 1956, several films produced just before it were shelved, certain film-makers did not work for years, and nor did some actors – the number one Hungarian film star, István Darvás, was jailed. It was many years before they could return to the studios, and the Hungarian cinema, which had played so influential a role in Eastern Europe in the early fifties, could resume its previous standing. The *oeuvre* of some directors (Mariassy, Fabry) was to be irreparably damaged by this brutal interruption, and it required a new generation of film-makers to come up with another original contribution.

The Poles, who followed with what was known as the 'Polish school' after 1955, lasted longer, but the movement was stopped in the early sixties, and two of its most talented members – Polanski and Skolimowksi – have since worked mainly abroad. The most famous victim of the changed circumstances was Skolimowski's satire of Stalinism in Poland, *Hands Up!*, which was never shown, although it now seems that there is a possibility it may reach the screens in Poland more than 15 years after it was made. Skolimowski has recently expressed the wish to shoot some additional footage.

In Czechoslovakia, the liberalization was to last the longest, being effected in two instalments. The first, from 1955 to 1958, produced some important films by Ladislav Helge, Vojtech Jasný, Zbynek Brynych, and the successful team of Jan Kadár and Elmar Klos (who were later to make the Oscar-winning *Shop on Main Street*). This shorter of the two 'liberal' periods came to an abrupt end at a special conference in the Slovak city of Kosice, after which Kadár and Klos's already completed *Three Wishes* was shelved before it could be publicly shown. When released many years later, its biting satire had lost a great deal of its edge.

The second period began in 1961 and lasted until 1969, a year after the Soviet occupation of the country. It is something of a paradox that some of the most interesting and politically controversial films ever shot in Eastern Europe, which were started in the brief interlude of freedom Czechoslovakia experienced in the Spring of 1968, were only finished following the Soviet invasion, ie in the autumn of that year or in early 1969. Some were to enjoy a brief release, others were withdrawn immediately before they could be shown. Later, the new Husák regime published a long list of films produced in the sixties and now unwanted, and a shorter one of films, forbidden forever, which included Milos Forman's delightful *Fireman's Ball.*

In Yugoslavia, the crushing of the liberal intellectual and artistic movement in the early seventies put paid to the most successful 'New Film' movement, two of whose leading representatives – Dusan Makavejev and Alexander Petrovich – had been working abroad ever since. Makavejev's famous *Mysteries of the Organism* has never been released in his native land.

Limited distribution

In East Germany and Bulgaria, short spells of liberalization have invariably been followed by long periods of rigidity. As a consequence, cases of shelved films and interrupted careers of promising film-makers are quite numerous. Again, some of these films came to be shown in later years, by which time they would miss their point (East Germany), or they would be completed only after long delays, their authors having had to change direction in the meantime (Vulchanov in Bulgaria).

In Rumania, the most famous victim of post-production measures was the already mentioned film by Lucian Pintillie, *The Reconstruction,* whose author was never to return to film-making.

In the Soviet Union such incidents were repeated periodically throughout the sixties the most tragic case of a film censored after it had been completed, and its director persecuted, being that of Sergei Paradjanov. Following this case, scripts of films made in the various Soviet republics had once more to be vetted and approved in Moscow – a practice which had been discontinued after Stalin's death. Since the end of the sixties there has been little post-production censorship, this proving unnecessary as controversial projects rarely reach the production stage. Of course there are exceptions, like the films of Andrei Tarkovski, or the Georgian director, Iosseliani. Even in such cases a solution has now been found in limiting the film's exposure to the smallest possible number of cinemas in remote suburbs or by having them shown only in individual republics rather than nationwide.

As far as exports are concerned, two measures deserve mention. The first consists of exporting films produced in the different ethnic Soviet republics almost exclusively in Russian-dubbed versions, thus depriving them of an important artistic component. The other is not to allow the best and most original Soviet films to enter competitions for awards at international film festivals. This is to prevent such movies winning prestigious prizes which would then have to be reported in the Soviet press, giving added importance to a 'dubious' film-maker or a 'dangerous' trend (again, Tarkovski, Iosseliani, and a few others).

The production policy practised in post-invasion Czechoslovakia now makes censorship after the event superfluous. In the past 12 years only some three or four films of any originality have managed to reach the studio floor. Of these, both movies made by Vera Chytilová after her return to film-making following her exclusion, *The Apple Game* and *The Panel Story*, produced in the late seventies, ran into problems and obtained only the most limited release.

The situation in Poland is obviously completely different. While in the seventies, several pictures were produced, or were started, only to be shelved or their production halted later, today Polish cinema ranks as one of the two or three most important and original in Europe. This is likely to continue as long as the advantages of a nationalized film industry are used – as is now the case – with little or no interference from the State. Films shelved or left unfinished in the seventies will now most probably make their belated appearance in Polish cinemas.

China: A Hundred Flowers or Poisonous Weeds?

Isabel Hilton

The fate of artistic expression in the cinema in China has closely paralleled that of other arts, suffering from constant and severe fluctuations in official policy, used as a weapon between warring factions of the political leadership, alternately encouraged and suppressed. To describe the problems of workers in the Chinese film industry as simply those of censorship seems ludicrously mild in even the briefest examination of the vagaries of cultural policy since 1949.

As in the other arts, the early 1950s brought a steady assertion of Party control over wayward film-makers and the warning of the Hu Feng affair. (A veteran writer who demanded individual creative freedom in a long memorandum to the Party, Hu Feng was denounced in 1954 as an anti-Marxist and anti-Party element.) Nineteen fifty-six brought the encouragement of the Hundred Flowers movement ('let a hundred flowers bloom, a hundred schools of thought contend') which was followed in 1957 by the repression of the anti-Rightist movement. The early 1960s saw some liberalization, only to be followed by the devastation of the Cultural Revolution. Since 1976, liberalization has again been followed by the beginnings of repression.

These reversals the cinema has shared with the other arts. The importance the Chinese have historically attached to the arts and their consciousness of the power of artistic expression have made them always vulnerable to political repression and, conversely, frequently placed the arts in the forefront of progressive or revolutionary movements. The cinema in China has been particularly exposed. It has always been recognized as a powerful and potentially subversive force, either explicitly, through the message it carried, or implicitly through the seduction of its images. And since Mao's widow, Jiang Qing, worked as a film actress in Shanghai in the 1930s and later rose to power through her sustained attacks on the practitioners of culture, it is not surprising that the cinema has had a difficult time.

A glance at the products of the early years, particularly the 1930s and 1940s, reveals that the infant Chinese cinema, in spite of precarious financing and constant trouble with the KMT (Kuomintang or Nationalists) or Japanese censors, was capable of producing films which still stand comparison with others anywhere else in the world. Actors and actresses like Zhao Dan, Sun Daolin, Bai Yang, directors and writers like Xia Yan, Tian Han, and many others laid the artistic foundations.

By 1949, the situation was complicated. Of the three main centres of film production, Changchun, Peking and Shanghai, Changchun had been in Communist hands since the defeat of the Japanese in 1945, Peking was under KMT control, and many of Shanghai's film-makers had scattered to Yanan or to Hong Kong to escape first KMT, then Japanese censorship. Others were continuing to operate, and some Shanghai studios remained independent for a few years after liberation.

Serving the people

The conflicts which were to emerge in the 1950s were not entirely unforeseen. In 1942, Mao's talks at the Yanan Forum on Literature and Art, in which he laid down the basics of party policy towards the arts, had already induced protest from some writers. In 1949, the bureaucratic organs responsible for the administration of Mao's policy were set up. The ultimate responsibility for what appeared on China's screens rested with the Ministry of Culture, under which was created a Film Bureau, and the Department of Propaganda. Among its personnel was Jiang Qing.

The aims of the film industry were boldly stated: 'A film industry must be created which fully serves the interest of all the people an which speaks out clearly and truthfully on the burning questions of the day.' In 1950, the state plan was for 26 full-length features, 17 documentaries, 40 reprints of Soviet films and 50 films to be commissioned from private studios in Hong Kong and Shanghai. One of those, *The Life of a Peking Policeman*, from a short story by Lao She, was one of the first to run into trouble. Released in 1950, it was withdrawn soon afterwards.

It was another film released in 1950 which became the real cause célèbre of that and subsequent years. *The Inside Story of the Qing Court* was actually produced in the Yonghua studio in Hong Kong in 1948, written by Yao Ke and directed by Chu Shiling. The row about the film is instructive, since it illustrates an early battle in the war between Liu Shaoqi and Mao Zedong which was to break out with such devastating consequences 14 years later.

Mao's wife bans the dowager

The crux of the dispute lay in whether the Empress Dowager of the Qing dynasty, Zixi, had been right to suppress the Boxer Rebellion. Liu Shaoqi, it is claimed, argued that it was a patriotic act in that it saved China from foreign invasion. Mao argued that it was the counter-revolutionary suppression of a proletarian uprising. The stage version had already been banned, but the film was a success with audiences both in Hong Kong and China. When Jiang Qing saw it, as a member of the commission which also included Lu Dingyi and Zhou Yang, the chief cultural bureaucrat of China until the Cultural Revolution, she immediately objected to it and called a meeting to decide whether it should be shown. The meeting did not go well. Zhou Yang was against banning it and two historians whom she tried to commission to attack the film, evaded the task. Frustrated, Jiang Qing banned the film and returned to the subject later.

Jiang Qing was displeased by much of what she saw in 1950, including *Sons and Daughters of Korea* which she had revised after overcoming Zhou Yang's resistance. The conflict in which she played a crucial role was over the film *The Life of Wu Xun*. Released in December 1950, the film was shown all over the country and over 30 articles appeared in praise of it. It did not, however, meet with Jiang Qing's approval and it was withdrawn from circulation; but that was not the end of the story. Wu Xun was a beggar who lived in the late 19th century in Shandong. He managed to accumulate capital, by saving and investing the proceeds of his trade, until he reached a position of wealth and respectability. He then used his money to found schools for the poor, convinced that only education could save China.

Jiang Qing took the view that praising Wu Xun negated the primary struggle of the time – the overthrow of the landlord class by the peasants. Her campaign against the film took her, heavily disguised, on an eight-month investigation in Shandong producing reports on the historical background, uncovering, amongst other things, that Wu Xun had been a landlord in the course of his career and that his schools, for reasons she does not explain, were never open to the poor.

Mao backs Jiang Qing

As her campaign against the film gathered momentum, everyone associated with it was forced to make a self-criticism. In May 1951,

Mao wrote an editorial for the *People's Daily* which quickly dispelled any doubts the film-makers might have had about the gravity of their offence: 'The questions raised by Wu Xun are fundamental in character,' said the editorial ... 'to approve or tolerate such praise [of people like Wu Xun] ... means to approve or tolerate reactionary propaganda vilifying the revolutionary struggle of the peasants, the history of China and the Chinese nation ... The appearance of the film *Wu Xun*, and in particular the praise lavished on Wu Xun and the film, show the degree of ideological confusion reached in our country's cultural circles ...'

Why, might one ask, did this film attract such virulent condemnation? Mao Zedong provides the answer. 'Certain communists, who have reputedly grasped Marxism, warrant particular attention ... when they come across specific ideas contrary to history ... they lose their critical faculties. Is it not a fact that reactionary bourgeois ideas have found their way into the militant Communist Party?'

Everybody weighed in with criticism, including the director, Sun Yu, and ending with Zhou Yang who published an article entitled 'Ideas that offend against the people, art that offends against realism'. Even this did not prevent attacks on the film being revived repeatedly over the years, or Zhou Yang's early support of it being used as evidence against him in the Cultural Revolution. Nor did it save the career of Sun Yu, the director, who did not make another film until 1957. He made three films between 1957 and 1960, but came under further attack in the Cultural Revolution. The episode was important in Mao's campaign to persuade Chinese intellectuals to accept the Marxist line and the line of the Yanan forum. It also served as a convenient excuse to bring the responsible studio, Kun Lun, under state control.

The critics bloom

As Party control increased, the Propaganda Department ensured that the bulk of production took seriously its responsibilities towards praising socialism, attacking the KMT and the Americans in Korea. Like the other arts, the subdued atmosphere among film workers came to the notice of the Party in the mid-1950s and the leadership decided it was secure enough to try a little liberalization. In May of 1956, Mao made his famous Hundred Flowers speech and indicated at the Eighth Party Congress in September that it should become a movement. Lu Dingyi, then Chief of the Propaganda Department, acknowledged that both the sciences and the arts were stagnating and invited comment. Nobody was prepared for the deluge of criticism which followed. The

Hundred Flowers was marked in the film industry by the publication of a new cinema magazine which criticized bureaucratic control and called for more individual creativity.

Jiang's blight

Appalled by the state of disaffection the Hundred Flowers campaign had revealed, the authorities counter-attacked. As Jiang put it: 'The class enemies at home began to chime in with the Soviet revisionists.' On 17 April 1957, the anti-Rightist campaign was launched. Never slow to spot a trend, Zhou Yang wrote about the dangers of Chinese cinema being led back to the road of capitalism. The publication of the first history of Chinese cinema was cancelled. The argument over *Inside Story of the Qing Court*, which had reappeared first as an opera and then as a stage play, was revived and it was banned in all versions. The director, Liu Ban, whose satiric comedies had touched the nerves of the bureaucracy, was attacked for 'concealing his anti-Party sentiments under a mask of comedy', an attack which ended his career. Writing of this period, Xia Yan says, '[in previous campaigns] films' scriptwriters and directors were not held personally, accountable or persecuted for their errors'. The same was not true of the anti-Rightist purges of 1957, campaigns of vilification followed thick and fast. The 'Anti-Revisionist' and 'poisonous weeds' movements of 1958 and 1964 respectively aimed their attacks considerably wider and very many people were seriously wronged.

Encouraging film-makers

The Great Leap Forward, a fever which swept the whole country in 1958 and 1959 also raised the temperature of the film industry, which was not only called upon to treble production but also mobilized to produce eulogies of the efforts of others.

In 1960, Zhou Enlai made a speech encouraging film-makers to forget the troubles of the past and concentrate on their work. Individual movies continued to run into trouble, however, in particular a film script by Wu Yungyi. It was originally published in 1958 and attacked in 1960. It dealt with an incipient revolt by the workers of a brush factory.

But whatever troubles the industry had faced hitherto, they were as nothing compared to what was to come. The Cultural Revolution and the struggle for power between Mao Zedong and Liu Shaoqi are well documented and do not need repetition here. Culture was one of the principal weapons in the battle to bring down Liu Shaoqi, and when he fell, thousands fell with him. Everyone associated with the arts since

1949, including such powerful figures as Zhou Yang, was disgraced. Some spent years labouring in the countryside. Others committed suicide.

Jiang Qing the weed-killer

In the film industry, the first warnings came in 1964 when all screenings of foreign films made before 1949 were banned. The following year, Xia Yen, the writer and director, was denounced and banished to Sichuan. His film, *The Lin Family Shop* produced in 1959 was released for criticism and the attack extended to veteran writer Mao Dun, on whose story the film was based. He was dismissed from his post as Minister of Culture. *The History of the Development of Chinese Cinema*, finally published in 1963 to a lukewarm official reception, was suddenly blasted in the *People's Daily* in 1966 for its 'sweeping praise of 30s cinema'. By 1966, film production was virtually at a standstill, except for such paeans of praise as *Chairman Mao Joins the Millions of the Cultural Revolution's Army*. A list of 400 'poisonous weeds' was published, condemning at a stroke virtually the entire corpus of Chinese cinema. The era of Jiang Qing had arrived.

After the initial wave of releases of poisonous weeds, for criticism, China's screens went virtually blank. Adulatory documentaries about the Cultural Revolution and one or two earlier films (*Tunnel Warfare, Fighting North and South*) were shown, but the first feature films had to wait seven years – seven years in which the cultural diet of China consisted of a handful of 'model operas'. The first films were film versions of these, followed in 1973 by a few feature films so closely modelled on them in style as to be indistinguishable, but for the absence of singing.

For one of the clearest illustrations of the role of the cinema in the power struggles of the Chinese leadership, it is instructive to turn to the eventful year of 1976. It began with the death of Zhou Enlai, for years the only moderating influence left in Chinese politics. He had succeeded in rehabilitating Deng Xiaoping, who was widely expected to succeed him as Premier. But two other factions at the centre were to fight it out that year – the 'left' represented by the Gang of Four, and a third group represented by Hua Guofeng. In April, demonstrations in support of Deng Xiaoping were brutally suppressed and his second disgrace confirmed. Hua took over the Premiership and, having apparently eliminated the opposition from the right, ended the year by smashing that of the left, arresting the Gang of Four after Mao's death in September and taking his place as Mao's successor and Chairman of the Party.

'Let a single flower bloom'

In the spring and summer of 1976, the propaganda organs were still under the control of the Gang of Four and bent towards the attack of 'that unrepentant capitalist roader in the Party' Deng Xiaoping. Thus it was that the film *Spring Shoots* became a tool of this struggle. In April 1976 the Xinhua News Agency reported a new upsurge in literature and the arts, inspired by the example of model opera. Such a work was the film *Spring Shoots* which 'broke with old ideas and depicted the struggle against capitalist roaders as a reflection of the salient feature ... etc.' *Spring Shoots* was the first film to take the Cultural Revolution as its theme.

The film was released for 1 October 1975 when, according to the eulogies, 'it immediately began to demonstrate its role as a tool in the class struggle'. Deng Xiaoping walked out of it, denouncing it as ultra-leftist, and delivering himself of the famous line: 'Let a single flower bloom.' The film upset him, it was explained, because its target was the Party capitalist roaders. As a glimpse of the conditions under which the film industry was labouring in the Cultural Revolution, it was revealed that *Spring Shoots* had taken *seven years* to produce, with all concerned living and working in rural Zhejiang for much of that time. Proof of its correctness, it was claimed, were three hundred letters of approval received by the studio.

Hua on the tightrope

After the fall of the Gang of Four in October 1976, Hua Guofeng took up the reins of propaganda, and by the following year, *Spring Shoots* was under attack as a poisonous weed which had been rewritten by the Gang of Four. As they had been mobilized to praise, so the masses were mobilized to criticize: a poster put up in a Shandong commune said: 'Our literature and art should help to strengthen and not discard or weaken the leadership of the communist party.' Although the fall of the Gang of Four unleashed torrents of criticism of their policy in the cinema, it did not, immediately, bring much relief to the film industry. Hua Guofeng tried to strengthen his precarious position by presenting himself as the only true heir to Mao Zedong, which left him walking a propaganda tightrope. Whilst accusing the Gang of persecuting film workers, not without a certain justification, Hua also accused Jiang Qing of appropriating to herself the glory of the creation of the model operas – for which, he now claimed, she was not responsible!

Rehabilitating the survivors

In November 1976, Mao's Hundred Flowers quotation was again printed in the *People's Daily* and various films suppressed by the Gang began to emerge, accompanied by suggestions – in those letters from the masses – that not all the films produced before the Cultural Revolution were bad. As a supreme irony, a 1963 quotation from Mao was produced in support: 'What has been achieved in cinema, new poetry, folk songs and fine arts should not be underestimated'.

Thousands of cultural figures were rehabilitated, including the entire Ministry of Culture, a policy which reached its climax in the case of Comrade Liu Shaoqi. It had all been a mistake, it was announced, a 'frame-up'. There never had been a 'black line' in the arts. The pace of liberalization picked up. Zhao Dan's last film *Red Crag*, and the novel from which it was drawn, were released. By 1978 the Shanghai film studios had most of its former personnel back ... except, of course, for those who had died under persecution or committed suicide. In February 1978 the magazine *Chinese Literature* published the scenario of the film *Dr Norman Berthume in China*, a movie completed in 1964 – just in time to run into trouble for glorifying a foreigner. In the same month, at a reception in Peking, veteran survivors were on view: the directors Yu Lan and Zui Wei, the actress Zhang Ruifang, and the actor Zhao Dan. The atmosphere was full of enthusiasm; 1978 was a year of great promise for intellectual freedom both within and without official circles.

Democracy in art

China's writers and artists sharpened their pens yet again. Perhaps this time, with a China relatively stable and united under Deng, committed to modernization and liberalization, things would be different. In October 1978, the magazine *Wen Yi Bao* sponsored a scenarists' forum in which, with a haunting echo of the call of 30 years previously, the aim was once again bravery and honesty.

By the end of 1978, the Party was once more beginning to regret the liberalization. The Democracy Movement which had exploded on the streets had clearly gone too far. The arrest and trial of Wei Jingsheng was a clear signal of official alarm, but the turn of the official artistic circles was to come later, and the official backlash was resisted throughout 1979. In May 1979, the *People's Daily*, which played a liberal role throughout the year, complained, 'Some people are comfortable only with a uniformity of public opinion. Were the lessons of the Gang of Four not enough?' In October that year, writers demonstrated in Peking for democracy in art and in November, at the Writers' Congress, a lively and prophetic debate was held on whether artists were really safe from official revenge. Among the sceptics was the writer and film-maker Bai Hua, who was soon to discover that his anxieties were well founded.

Party backlash

By 1980, the two sides were clearly slugging it out in Peking. The arguments were wearily familiar. In favour of restriction, it was said that too many works were being produced which were flawed with too much emphasis on the negative side of life. The excuse of the quest for perfection, first criticized by China's only untouched literary hero, Lu Xun, in an attack on Party bureaucracy in the 1930s, and subsequently levelled at the methods of the Gang of Four, was once again in use as a means of censorship. In a major speech in January, Deng Xiaoping, forced into retreat by discontent in the Party, reminded people of the duty of the arts to encourage the march towards the four modernizations. A scriptwriters' meeting the following month took up the theme: such subjects, it was concluded, as juvenile delinquency and bureaucratic privilege could be tackled as long as sufficient attention was paid to those forces which struggled to overcome them.

It is worth looking at some of the products of this latest period of liberalization to see what it was which so alarmed the Party. Young writers had been quick to respond to the change in atmosphere and a number of film scripts were produced which tackled the dark side of Chinese society. Among them *In the Archives of Society* by Wang Qing, *The Girl Thief* by Li Kewei and *If I Were Real*, a stage play which was to have been adapted for the cinema, stand out.

In *Archives of Society*, the heroine turns to crime after being raped by a debauched army general and his son. She eventually arranges the death of her former love when he refused to join the gang she is in and when the crime is investigated, the policeman is horrified at what he discovers. He calls for everyone to be arraigned, but realizes it is hopeless. Asked what should be done with the records of his investigation, he replies: 'Destroy them. The fate of these notes can only be destruction. But all crimes remain inscribed in the archives of society, graven on the hearts of the victims.' He is then arrested himself.

The Girl Thief pursues a similar theme – that of a woman who turns to crime after seeing her mother tortured to death in the Cultural Revolution. *If I Were Real* was based on a real incident, in which a young man was arrested for impersonating the son of a high official. At his trial, he offered in his defence the thought that if he really had been the son of a high official, the extravagant luxuries and privileges he had enjoyed would not have been thought untoward.

In February 1980, it was announced that the filming of these three projects had been banned because 'they had serious errors, the world view is wrong, and they could have no artistic effect'.

The resistance to the backlash continued through 1980. In July, the *People's Daily* published a call for the persistence of the Hundred Flowers policy with a realistic account of the experience of artistic liberalization: 'The 24 years since the Hundred Flowers Movement have been a long and tortuous road: at first control ... very tight and rigid and the atmosphere tense. Then some call for the implementation of the Hundred Flowers. Once the atmosphere is activated, some are unhappy and displeased ... and call for a counter-attack. This cycle has been repeated many times. Our past mistake was that we took the Hundred Flowers as no more than expediency and failed to apply it as a long-term basic policy.'

That is the question

The *People's Daily* complaint was dramatically illustrated in October by the intervention in the debate of one of the greatest cinema actors of all time Zhao Dan who made his name in Shanghai in the 1930s and when Shanghai fell to the Japanese in 1937, toured with anti-Japanese agitprop. He was imprisoned by a local warlord in Shanxi for five years, released in 1943 and returned to Shanghai after the war. He was criticized in the 1950s for attempting to restore 'bourgeois literary films', and imprisoned again, for five years, during the Cultural Revolution. Released in 1973, he went back to work in 1976. In 1980, he was dying of cancer. In September, a month before he died, he wrote a moving plea for artistic freedom which the *People's Daily* published on 8 October, two days before his death.

Commenting on the renewed calls for strengthening Party leadership over the arts, Zhao Dan wrote: 'Past experience has taught the artists that in every such strengthening process there will be much physical and mental suffering and flagrant interference.... The Party can lead in formulating national economic plans and agricultural policy ... why should the Party tell us how to farm, how to make a stool, or how to fry vegetables? Why should they instruct writers how to write or actors how to act? For example, in shooting the film *Lu Xun*, I have grown or shaved off my beard several times since the tests in 1960. Twenty years have passed and the film has still not been shot ... If works have to be checked and approved at all levels, no good ones will

Plate 1 Patricio Guzmán's *Poder Popular* ('The Power of the People')

Plate 2 Pier Paolo Pasolini's *Salo*. BFI Stills, Posters and Designs

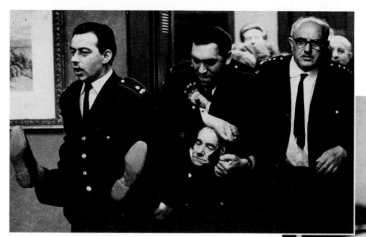

Plate 3 *(top)* Milós Forman's *The Firemen's Ball*.
National Film Theatre

Plate 4 *(below)* Jorge Sanjinés's *El Coraje del
Pueblo* ('The Courage of the People'). © The Other
Cinema

Plate 5 *(right)* Tengiz Abuladze's *Repentance*.
Canon Releasing

Plate 6 *(below right)* Andrzej Wajda. *The Guardian*

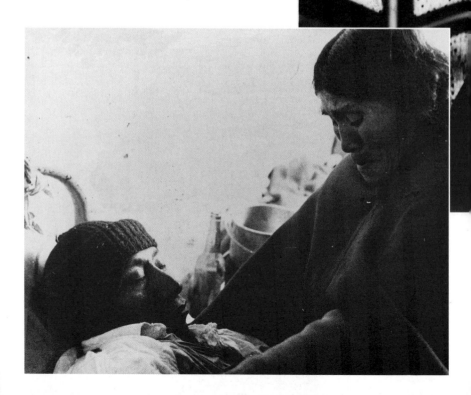

Plate 7 Hitler and Leni Riefenstahl on set, 1935: *A Triumph of Wills*. BFI Stills, Posters and Designs

Plate 8 Sergei Eisenstein's *Battleship Potemkin*. BFI Stills, Posters and Designs

Plate 9 Lucio Fulci's *Zombie Flesh Eaters.* The Alan Jones Collection

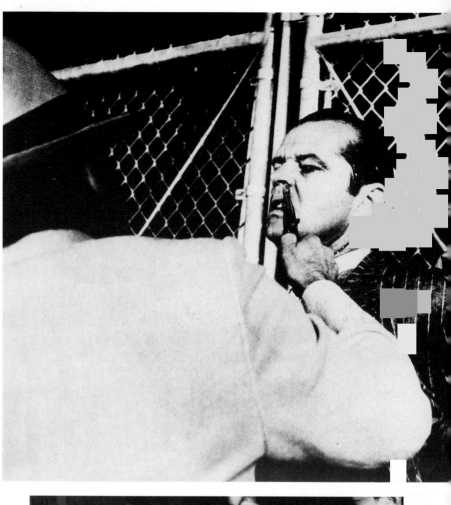

Plate 10 *(left)* Roman Polanski's *Chinatown*. BFI Stills, Posters and Designs

Plate 11 *(below left)* Zhang Yuan (centre) during the making of *Erzi* ('Sons') in 1995. Photo, Tony Rayns

Plate 12 *(below)* Arthur C. Clarke. Victor Gollancz

Plate 13 *(bottom)* Stanley Kubrick's *2001: A Space Odyssey*. BFI Stills, Posters and Designs

Plate 14 Haile Gerima. Photo, Justin Williams.

Plate 15 Haile Gerima's *Sankofa.* BFI Stills, Posters and Designs

be produced ... I no longer have anything to lose by speaking openly. I have been long-winded enough, and what is the use of my words ...?' (Written on my sickbed, September 1980).

Zhao Dan's article appears to have been the last straw for elements in the Party grown impatient with criticism. In December 1980, the Minister of Culture, Huang Zhen, was replaced. Early this year, the *People's Daily* was criticized for publishing the article and 1981 has brought renewed attacks on 'negative' films. The chief target has been the writer and film-maker, Bai Hua, whose anxieties about the safety of artists from persecution in 1979 now appear prophetic. His film *The Son and the Man*, originally titled *Bitter Love*, tells the story of a Chinese artist who returns to China in the 1950s, only to be persecuted in the Cultural Revolution. He takes to the wilds and lives there, but when his friends come looking for him to tell him of the fall of the Gang of Four, he mistakes their approaching voices for a signal that his sufferings are about to be renewed. Fleeing in the snow, he collapses and dies, his footsteps forming a giant question-mark.

The film was shown briefly at the end of last year, then withdrawn amid criticism of its ending. In April this year, Bai Hua was accused in the official press of trying to blacken the image of the nation, of Mao and the Communist Party. As the crackdown proceeds, Zhou Yang, that great weather-vane of cultural policy, criticized the 'liberal tendencies of writers who follow their consciences rather than the Party'. But perhaps the most succinct statement of the official view of the proper place of film-makers has come from Hu Qiaomu, a member of the Central Secretariat and President of the Chinese Academy of Social Sciences. 'It is stupid,' he remarked, 'to have dictatorship and not to exercise it.'

What flowers can blossom under the renewed dictatorship remains to be seen. In spite of the vagaries of cultural policy, Chinese film-makers continue trying to produce films worthy of their talents. The most recent crop include some powerful melodramas on recent history and a new generation of writers has appeared. But the close attention paid to the products of the film industry has left it no time to deal with the inherent problems of organization and finance. It would be wrong to assume that the new severity in the official line has reached, or even threatens to reach, the level of the Cultural Revolution or even the Anti-Rightist Movement, but the liberty of the late 1970s is already over. There is a certain irony in the quiet reappearance in Peking of Hu Feng, nearly 30 years after his disgrace for calling for artistic freedoms, just as those who call for them now are coming under renewed pressure to uphold the values of patriotism and Party leadership.

Special acknowledgement to Jay Leyda's book *Diangying* (MIT Press, 1972) and to the British Film Institute Dossier *Electric Shadows: Chinese Cinema*, edited by Tony Rayns and Scott Meek..

Latin America: Generals, Civilians and Cinema

Homero Alsina Thevenet

A true understanding of Latin American culture, cinema, and film censorship is often hindered by simplification and generalization. The first thing a European or North American observer must be asked to accept is that the truth cannot be contained in a few sentences or general concepts, because Latin America is made up of many countries stretching over a vast territory, with different histories and striking contrasts between them. As well as backwardness and misery there are huge modern cities such as Buenos Aires, São Paulo, Mexico, Brasilia; side by side with illiteracy there are the works of writers such as Jorge Luis Borges, Pablo Neruda, Gabriel García Marquez, or Mario Vargas Llosa, together with an Argentinian who in 1970 won the Nobel Prize for chemistry – Luis F. Leloir. The superficial reader of brief press reports on Latin America will see everything in terms of simple contrasts: on one side there are guerrillas (as in Cuba, Nicaragua, or El Salvador), on the other military or dynastic dictatorships; such as those of Stroessner (Paraguay), Trujillo (Dominican Republic), the Somozas (Nicaragua) or Batista (Cuba). But this view, because it is partially correct, obscures the varied paths of history and the quieter times of civilian rule. For most of this century Uruguay, for example, achieved advances in democracy (and also in social legislation, education, and freedom of the press) which led to its being known as the 'Switzerland' of Latin America. Some countries have seen *coups d'état* every Tuesday afternoon (as in Bolivia), whereas in others (Mexico, for example) there has been remarkable stability.

The culture of Latin America should be analysed with the same caution as its political and social reality. A handful of countries

(Argentina, Brazil, Mexico, and to a lesser extent Venezuela) have been able to support national book and film industries. Possibilities for the exchange of this culture, however, have been rare, not only because of the small amount spent on cultural affairs in the continent, but also because of the various divisions which have led to the region being termed with 'disunited states of the south'. It is difficult to organize theatre tours, and ever-present industrial, commercial, and customs barriers prevent books or films crossing frontiers.

Moreover, there are the problems created for vulnerable societies by the operation of the free market economy, which tends to lead to the domination of the weak by the strong. When Latin Americans talk about imperialism – and 'North American imperialism' is certainly a phrase which is heard daily – they do not necessarily mean abusive interventions by the United States in the Dominican Republic, Cuba, Nicaragua or Chile. More often they are referring to the effects of imported technology and investments made in Latin America by more powerful countries. They mean the absorption of raw materials by foreign capital, the English railways which so upset Peron in Argentina, German chemical industries – or the vast network of communications deriving from the US, which takes in radio, television, telecommunications agencies, the press and cinema. Such interests have always found excellent partners in a minority of Latin Americans, as they still do, thus helping to maintain élites enjoying great fortune and privilege, and to nurture opposition, including the guerrillas. It is too easy, however, to blame all the continent's ills on foreign intervention; the military regimes, police repression and torturers have come from among the Latin American peoples themselves. Moreover, it should be pointed out that, however noble its motives, opposition to oppression has itself sometimes led to questionable and even catastrophic consequences. Revolutionary Cuba has known grave episodes of imprisonment, flight and exile. Guerrillas in Argentina and Uruguay have killed innocent people and provided pretexts for violent repression. Peron's government decayed into demagoguery, corruption and dictatorship.

In Europe it is the 'political cinema' of Latin America which is best known, partly because its makers (such as Glauber Rocha, or Fernando Solanas) have sought this outlet, partly thanks to a particularly coherent production effort (in Cuba), and partly because the European public and critics are attracted to a cinema dealing in violent and primitive themes. This last was the reason that European film festival juries awarded first prizes to *Orfeo Negro* ('Black Orpheus'), by Marcel Camus at Cannes in 1959, *O Pagador de Promessas* ('The Given Word') by Anselmo Duarte (Cannes, 1962) and

Martin Fierro by Torre Nilsson (Rio de Janeiro, 1969). Alongside this branch of the art, however, there has always been an abundant entertainment cinema, offering both comedy and drama, which reached its height in Mexico and Argentina between 1940 and 1960. Without this cinema the work of Emilio Fernandez, Leopoldo Torre Nilsson, or the Latin American films of Luis Buñuel could not have existed. These film industries go through recurring periods of crisis, due mainly to lack of sales abroad. For example, although it shares the same language, Spain does not buy Latin American films.

In Latin America itself there is a remarkable awareness of foreign cinema, although in Central America this is confined largely to Hollywood (in Cuba it covers many different cinemas, but little Hollywood). Argentina, Brazil, Mexico, and especially Uruguay, have been the centres for a deep, though in some senses second-hand, film culture. Between 1945 and 1970 these countries could generally enjoy, perhaps even more than in Europe, most of past cinema: together with Italian neo-realism, the new waves in British, French, Soviet, and Czechoslovak cinema, the work of Bergman, Antonioni, Fellini, Wajda or Kurosawa.

Repression

By far the most notorious and frequent censorship of cinema in Latin America has been that of the military against film-makers who sought to create socially committed works. In 1969 government repression forced Glauber Rocha to leave Brazil; in 1971 Jorge Sanjinés quit Bolivia following Banzer's coup; Pinochet's 1973 takeover in Chile led to a widespread exodus of film directors (such as Miguel Littín, Patricio Guzmán, Pedro Chaskel, Helvio Soto, Raúl Ruiz; the 1976 military coup in Argentina brought prison and probable death for the film director Raymundo Gleyzer, and meant exile for Fernando Solanas, Octavio Getino, Gerardo Vallejo, Jorge Cedrón, Nicholás Sarquis, and Lautaro Murúa, together with actors such as Héctor Alterio, Marilina Ross, and Luis Politti. Some of these film-makers managed to rescue their material, put it together in exile, and show it; some were able to take up their careers again in other countries. This renewal of activity in exile has led to films like Guzmán's *La Batalla de Chile* ('The Battle of Chile'), Littín's *Actas de Marusia* ('Letters from Marusia') and Solanas's *Los Hijos de Fierro* ('The Sons of Fierro'). Through these and other films, cinema has joined in the great movement of Latin American culture in exile. At the same time, censorship in each of these countries has reached its worst. Torre Nilsson quickly became aware of it when what was to be his last film,

Piedra Libre ('Free for All'), was temporarily banned in Argentina in April 1976, a month after the military coup. Distributors, cinema managers, and the public became aware of it when not only all Russian and Czechoslovak films disappeared, but also those from Western Europe which strayed into eroticism or politics; prohibitions affected directors from Bertolucci to Jancsó, from Pasolini to Makavejev. Previously released films also fell victim to censorship. The Uruguayan government banned Pontecorvo's *Battle of Algiers* in October 1968 because they saw it as indirectly condoning the Tupamaro guerrillas who were very active at that time; over the next ten years both old and new political films vanished from view in many countries, from Eisenstein's *Potemkin*, to *State of Siege* by Costa-Gavras.

But this censorship is only part of the story. It should be borne in mind that film censorship is just one aspect of a more general repression, directed above all against books and journalism (see Andrew Graham-Yooll, *The Press in Argentina 1973–8*, Writers and Scholars Educational Trust, London, 1979). It is also worth remembering that film censorship is mainly one of *omission*, and can pass by unnoticed. As the film industry involves high costs, and since internal distribution inside Latin America is not profitable enough, private capital has been unwilling to take the risk. State support for the film industry has become inevitable: money for production, a guaranteed showing for a certain proportion of nationally produced films, help with the import of material, and with the shooting of films, plus a whole string of permits, pressures, and controls has become necessary. This is where censorship begins. It is obvious in those industries outside Latin America which are under direct state control (the Soviet Union, Czechoslovakia, Hungary, Poland), where a project that the government does not like quite simply does not get made, leaving very little which can be said, and few places in which to say it. In Latin America, something similar has occurred with the state film monopoly in Cuba, which led many prominent directors, writers, and photographers to leave the island (among them Eduardo Manet, Roberto Fandiño, Guillermo Cabrera Infante, Néstor Almendros). And the same thing has been happening increasingly elsewhere in Latin America, where the victim of censorship is now not so much the film which is not shown, but the film which is never made. The results of this are obvious. Whilst European cinema abounds in eroticism and pornography almost to excess, whereas the miraculous Wajda can make his socially pointed films in Poland, whilst Hollywood can permit itself films criticizing the army and the police, or which discuss such crucial themes as

Watergate or Vietnam, today's Latin American cinema has inevitably become superficial, aiming solely to entertain.

Roots in the past

It would however be a great mistake to imagine that the military regimes invented censorship in Latin America. Its roots lie in the previous civilian governments, just as current social and political realities have their origins in earlier events.

- In 1962 Jorge Sanjinés and his group made *Revolución* ('Revolution'), a documentary about Bolivian society. It was banned by president Paz Estenssoro, because he found that 'the uniforms of his guard were too much like those of repressive troops which were shown on the screen'. Yet Paz Estenssoro was a liberal president.
- The cinema in Argentina, Bolivia, Brazil, Chile, Colombia, and Peru, has been hit by bans and cuts for the greater part of this century, under both military and civilian governments, usually carried out by organizations such as the 'National Film Control Boards'.
- The most notorious censor in Argentina, Miguel P. Tato, famous both for the ferocity of his censorship and the length of his tenure of office (1974 to 1978, spanning both civilian and military regimes) was appointed by a civilian Peronist government.
- In 1968, under Ongania's military regime in Argentina, Fernando Solanas and Octavio Getino completed (in near clandestinity) *La Hora de los Hornos* ('The Hour of the Furnaces'), which called for a popular Peronist revolt against the dictatorship. The film was shown in semi-secrecy within Argentina, and widely screened abroad. It ended with a sequence devoted to Che Guevara. In 1973 the Peronists did return to power, and *La Hora de los Hornos* was finally shown publicly in Buenos Aires. However, its makers had cut the sequence with Che Guevara; it seems that once back in power, Peron did not want to hear about any further revolutions against social injustice.
- Nor did the Peronist government approve of *Los Traidores* ('The Traitors'), an excellent fictional film apparently made by Raymundo Gleyzer, although his name does not appear in the credits. It strongly attacked corruption among trade union leaders, which was a historic fact. The film could only be screened privately in Argentina from 1974 to 1976, and was subsequently confiscated by the military government (which probably explains the disappearance or death of Gleyzer in 1976).

- In 1921 the Argentine army brutally suppressed a peasant revolt in the south. Osvaldo Bayer later wrote a book about the episode, called *Los Vengadores de la Patagonia Trágica* ('The Avengers of Tragic Patagonia'). In 1973, in the first months of Peronist 'liberalization', Hector Olivera made an excellent, objective version of the historical events entitled *La Patagonia Rebelde* ('Rebel Patagonia'). By 1974 the Peronist government had moved to the right, and the first screening of the film was held up for several months due to pressure from the military. In 1976 Videla's military regime took power. Olivera himself, his associate Fernando Ayala, and the film distributors Aries now claim that *La Patagonia Rebelde* does not exist, and do not even include it in their catalogues: an effective form of censorship, and one which makes all paper-work unnecessary.

Ousmane Sembene and *Ceddo*

Malcolm Coad

A significant novelist before turning in his early forties to film-making, Ousmane Sembene is Africa's leading director. He was born in 1923 of a poor family in southern Senegal, travelling to France at the age of 15 when he joined up with the Tirailleurs Senegalais, a force formed by the French to fight the Germans at the beginning of World War II. As A. Mactar Gueye has pointed out, it was 'while enduring the harsh life of an immigrant [that] Sembene became politicised, staunchly anti-colonist, and an active trade unionist'. His experiences as a black worker in Marseilles are the force behind his first novel, *Docker Noir* ('Black Docker'), published in 1957. Five more novels followed before his first feature film, *La Noire de* ... ('Black Girl') in 1966, which was also the first full-length feature to be made by a black African.

Sembene is a passionate film-maker, a Marxist, and uncompromising in his denunciation of colonialism and more modern forms of economic and cultural domination of Africa from abroad. His 1972 feature *Emitai* caused outrage in official circles in France for its portrayal of the treatment of southern Senegalese villagers by French military authorities. At the same time, however, his vision is subtle, ironic and unrhetorical. While affirming his socialism, he constantly refuses to lay down easy prescriptions for his continent's complex problems. He describes his task as rather to 'reveal' the roots and sources of Africa's identity, and therefore of its future, and thereby to help his people to 'recognize' themselves, the more completely to construct that future. 'If others undervalue us,' he said in an interview in *Framework* magazine (no 7/8, Spring 1978), 'that has no further significance for us. Africa must get beyond deriving everything from the European view.' But he argues also that Africa 'cannot return to the past'. The deep penetration of traditional African society by elements from outside – notably by certain values instilled by Christianity and

Islam – is not only an historical fact, but has in many ways enriched the 'synthesis' that is contemporary African society. Africa must therefore 'recognize the problems of the whole world' and claim its place proudly in that world: a process which will involve sifting the good and the bad in its traditions, and settling accounts not only with colonialism but also with the corrupt black bourgeoisies which now wear the mantles of power doffed at independence by the colonialists themselves.

It is these black bourgeoisies, and their predecessors, the tribal leaders who co-operated in the past with the slavers, against whom Sembene's criticism is most particularly directed. Hence the ambiguous position he occupies in his home country, where he is a highly respected national figure, but where also substantial cuts were made by the Senegalese Board of Film Censorship in his 1974 feature *Xala*, while his latest film, *Ceddo* has been banned outright. The ostensible reason for the prohibition was that the spelling of the title contravenes a decree by President Leopold Senghor (himself a distinguished poet) on spelling in indigenous languages. More likely, however, is that the film as a whole ran foul of the country's political, cultural and religious establishment, which Sembene has described as composed of 'politburo, censor and inquisition'. The final decision, he believes, was taken by the first of these: 'In the case of my film, it wasn't the censor but the politically responsible group who were decisive ... The control exercised by the bourgeoisie over film is even stronger than in colonial times ... Perhaps they want to support a certain kind of cinema. But a cinema asking questions, raising problems – that they do not want' (*Framework*).

The banning reflects the complexity of the issues discussed above and Sembene's place within them. *Ceddo* discusses the role played by Islam, and to a lesser extent by Catholicism, in Senegal in the epoch of slavery. The issue at stake is less the precepts of any particular religion as such than the political significance and form of its imposition, and its distortion in the interests of domination: in this case by a dictatorial Imam over a divided and uncertain tribal aristocracy and rebellious villagers. It seems that Senegal's modern authorities saw implications in this for themselves and the foreign economic interests at work in the country in the late twentieth century. Religious leaders, meanwhile, perceived an attack on Islam itself – not least in the unthinkable killing of the Imam by a woman, Princess Dior (a denouement which demonstrates another of Sembene's principal concerns: the strength and will of women in African society).

Anti-*Repentance*

Karel Kyncl

Two East German newspapers, the party organ *Neue Deutschland* (30 October 1987) and the youth paper *Junge Welt* (28 October), carried unusually harsh reviews of the surrealistic, anti-Stalinist Soviet film *Repentance* by the Georgian director Tengiz Abuladze. The film was conspicuously absent from the recent 'Festival of Soviet Films in the GDR' but had earlier been shown on West German television, which is received by over 80 per cent of East German households. (An effective way to overcome censorship in the special German situation.)

The film, wrote Dr Harald Wessel, a deputy editor-in-chief of *Neues Deutschland*, was pessimistic, 'seeing and painting everything black'. This 'nihilistic picture [was] untrue, inhumane, and lacking in perspective', he said. Indeed, it was a 'stone-age view mocking all those millions of people who unselfishly fought and risked their lives for mankind's progress'.

Writing in *Junge Welt*, Hans-Dieter Schuett, the paper's editor-in-chief and a member of the party youth organization's secretariat, called the film a 'work of exaggerated symbolism' that 'undermines the basis for an honest evaluation of the issues involved'. He argued that the assumption conveyed by the film 'that among every three persons there are four enemies becomes a mocking denunciation of revolutionary vigilance'. He saw in the film 'horrible visions of a satanic system, which I perceive as a fatalistic submission to the inevitability of the misuse of power, denunciation, and terror ... The impression that Abuladze's parable conveys to me is of concave reflection of a fundamentally flawed world; and this historical and philosophical blackening in the end blackens the reputation of Marxist-Leninist historiography.'

Well, as far as 'blackness' of the said historiography is concerned, only a month ago we quoted two articles from the unofficial Soviet bulletin *Glasnost* dealing with the systematic official destruction of historical documentary evidence from the 1930s, 40s and 50s, with the 'destruction of memory'. And one can very well imagine how East German journalists would treat mountains of evidence of the Stalinist 'misuse of power, denunciation and terror', if they were allowed to describe it in any other way than 'anti-Soviet slander': one of the basic works of the reputed Marxist-Leninist historiography – the *Great Soviet Encyclopaedia* – brings in its three different editions three distinctly different versions of the Stalin era, and thus enables the party propagandists to delete whatever 'does not apply' at the given time.

Nevertheless, this is not exactly the point: *Repentance* is not historiography, but a work of art. The *Soviet* film director presents in it *his* personal view on a situation *he* and people in *his* country had lived through – and it seems almost unbelievable that, of all people, two East German propagandists have the arrogance to lecture him on 'nihilism', 'historical untruth', 'inhumanity' or 'lacking in perspective'. It can only be explained by a special notion of art which – despite *glasnost* – is still maintained by Communist hardliners in the GDR and elsewhere: namely that art – to quote Schuett again – is 'obliged to struggle against views that are alien and harmful to socialism'. This very notion leads, of course, to ideological censorship, the burning of books and the imprisonment of creative people.

On a more obvious level, the articles in *Neues Deutschland* and *Junge Welt* were attempts to counter the influence of the West German media on East German society. In doing so, however – Barbara Donovan from *RFE Research* comments – they posed some delicate questions about the current relationship between the East German and Soviet Communist Parties. Soviet Minister of Foreign Affairs Eduard Schevernadze, it should be recalled, expressed his approval of the film *Repentance* during his tenure as party chief in Georgia. At two points Schuett quoted a *Pravda* article on Stalin by Leonid Kurin, thereby implying that his position was also the Soviet one. And the reviews appeared a week before the Soviet leader Mikhail Gorbachev was due to speak on the 70th anniversary of the October revolution. As his speech was apparently approved in advance at the CPSU CC plenum on 21 October, it is possible that the East German leadership was given prior notice that Gorbachev's speech would, contrary to widespread expectation, be cautious in addressing the Soviet past and would follow the established party line. This may have encouraged the East Germans to publish two pieces criticizing the film.

Pinochet and I

An interview with the Chilean film-maker who secretly returned from exile to make a clandestine film about the state of Chile

Miguel Littín

The military government in Chile plans to continue in power. According to its 1980 Constitution, at the end of 1988 there is to be a plebiscite to approve one single candidate (probably Pinochet) who will be President for eight years. Political opponents have to decide whether to join in this game, or stay outside and face repression.

Recent legislation punishes those belonging to any Marxist-inspired political group, or reporting opinions or ideas related to Marxism. Marxism (or its supposed synonyms Communism and Socialism) means everything that is un-Chilean; it is blamed for all the violence and social tension. Against Allende's 'Chilean road to Socialism', Pinochet offers the traditional values of Chilean society, free from corrupting 'foreign' influences.

This attitude is particularly noticeable in culture. General Pinochet lauds the national dance, the cueca, *and claims responsibility for saving national traditions. Meanwhile Chilean television and cinemas have been opened to world markets, national film-making has been neglected, and the result is that of 3,000 feature films shown in the past decade, only 10 were made in Chile.*

This conservative and falsely traditional culture has been opposed inside and outside Chile by a generation of writers, film directors, and others. Many of them first emerged during Allende's 1971–73 Popular Unity government, when there were efforts to revive culture and involve as many people as possible in its production and enjoyment.

Those who were forced into exile in 1973 discovered a new world. Their experiences enriched their work, but nevertheless the vast majority wish for nothing so much as to reintegrate themselves with the Chile to which they still remain passionately attached. Pinochet's government forbids them entry, brands them 'dummies of international Marxism', and even threatens their lives or livelihoods.

Littín visited London in November 1987 to give a lecture at the National Film Theatre: he talked to Ros Bain.

You are working on a film in Nicaragua at the moment?

Yes, on the life of Sandino. I've been reading about him for the past year to try and find the human qualities of the historic characters, the psychological make-up of Sandino, because I don't want a stereotype hero distinct from other people. I want to find – behind all the books of documents – the real human being and his motives. It is very easy to ask why Sandino fought and answer 'For independence and freedom', but these are just sentences, words. I want to find the profound reasons as to why a man fights, loves and lives, and explain this.

Does Nicaragua bring back memories of Allende's Chile?

There is something, perhaps something about the enthusiasm; it's the participation of young people that I think is similar. However, Nicaragua has its own strong attraction. They are a very special people, with their own human micro-climate in which things are very different. Things are not black or white; there are always nuances. Each people has its own particular characteristics. The Nicaraguans seem a very transparent people with whom it's easy to establish a dialogue and understanding. Also, what you notice is the love of life that explodes everywhere. These things don't depend just on the political super-structure but on the make-up of the people.

What remains in your memory about your visit to Chile two years ago?

A terrible nostalgia. A surge of nostalgia against which I have to fight very strongly because it is always with me, in my dreams, or when I wake up in hotel rooms. It is always there: the mountains, the people, the space that is the personal universe of a human being.

Have you any chance of being allowed back in?

No. There seems to be a very strong incompatibility between the film-maker Miguel Littín and the Dictator Augusto Pinochet. I don't understand why a person like myself, a film-maker, can't be allowed in when they authorize the entry of important political people or people who have had an important role in the past, ex-ministers, senators and so on. Of course I'm very happy that they can enter, because they have invigorated the political situation.

Now it seems that there are threats against people whose work in the Chilean theatre under the dictatorship is the most outstanding and important. They are very courageous people who have risked everything to produce quality theatre, which has gone beyond showing plays by Miller, Pinter etc (universal culture). They have also developed Chilean theatre, which has denounced the regime, naturally, and also expressed what is happening in society around them. Now an ultra-right paramilitary commando with the name of Trizano has been formed to threaten these people. Few Chileans will have heard of this man Trizano: he was an officer who murdered many indigenous people of Araucania. He was, practically, in charge of exterminating the Araucanians on behalf of the Chilean government. So this dark name is only known by the bloody deeds that were perpetrated against the indigenous people. They said there should be a Chilean culture without any foreign elements in it. This had a precedent two weeks earlier, when Pinochet announced that the *cueca* – the dance – would have disappeared if it hadn't been for the military coup. Because during the times of *Unidad Popular*, Chile was penetrated by foreign culture.

And do you believe you can't go back because of a personal problem with the Junta?

No. It is evidently something political. But it is interesting that the dictatorship is so frightened of cultural people. They fear a film-maker and above all they fear the people from the theatre who now face death threats. They are frightened of ideas, because they know deep down that ideologically speaking, in the realm of ideas and feelings, they have lost the battle. And they are frightened that people may express themselves by means of a stage, newspaper or film, because it shows that there are people ready to contest the regime's ideas.

Did you find there was much film-making when you were in Chile two years ago?

You have to remember that in 1973 culture, especially the cinema, was totally razed. Nearly all film-makers died, went into exile, or disappeared. So people took a long time trying to build an alternative and it is only in the last few years that they have managed to form new groups. They have made feature films and many documentaries. They have expressed themselves particularly in video and this is how they have solved problems of cost and distribution. They have organized alternative distributors for the videos so now there are as many good quality Chilean films as there are foreign, and they have a cinema which is called Biografo where they can be shown. Let's not talk about these people solely in a political context. These are people who have learnt how to survive and bring out a cultural alternative and this is how they exist and why they are strong. These are people who have formed cinema workshops, who work in the Catholic university. They are people who, 20 years ago when the first Latin American film festival was held, perhaps had nothing to do with the cinema but who, despite 14 years of dictatorship, have revived the Chilean cinema.

Would you really like to go back and participate in this or do you feel that after 14 years away you could now not return?

The only thing I really want to do is to go back. Remember all the risks I took to return clandestinely. I didn't just go back, I made a film and let it be known that I was there. It was a way of recuperating my identity. My being and identity is intimately linked to that small piece of land which lies between the mountains and the sea, Chile. I would return immediately if I could.

Some exiles have said that they would not go back to a country of torturers and collaborators; that it is not the same country as before.

The trauma of exile is very complicated and one has to understand it in all its facets. The majority deny the possibility of going back because they know they can't. You cannot live with a packed suitcase. People need to put down roots, to build an everyday existence around them. Children need to go to school, make friends. Life needs to be formed and there is something more important than one's homeland, and all those words, and that is life itself. So people have a duty and obligation to defend their life and build their ordinary lives. I know many people have problems with their children because they have grown up away from Chile. So when their parents say 'We're going to go back to Chile', it's like beginning a second exile. Many people, if they do go back, won't have any work. And you can't just return saying 'Here I am, *patría mía*, what shall I do?' So what is needed is a re-education in order to go back; it isn't easy. There are some people who *can* return easily and who after two days are back in the flow of things. I also know of painful cases, such as a friend who was there for one week and committed suicide because he had dreamt of a utopia which didn't exist; when he had to face reality he couldn't take it. Exile isn't only the physical fact of being away from one's country, but an emotional and human break.

What's happening to the new Latin American cinema?

It is still an adolescent. It is at a moment when it has to make big decisions. In the 1960s it had links with the political fights of the continent – with Che in Bolivia and the rise of the popular movement in Chile; the continent was inspired by the Cuban revolution, the student turmoil in Mexico. In 1968 the whole continent was boiling, white hot, and in the middle of social and political struggle, with students in the street etc, with all these ideas and all this strength, an awareness was created. Over the last 20 years much has fallen by the wayside, a lot has disappeared, virtually a whole generation, victims of repression, the reaction of the Right, the military coups, but our cinema has managed to come through it all. It hasn't closed itself off but has managed to open up to other tendencies in Latin America. I don't think this is the moment when it can be closely defined. Many people might disagree with what I'm saying; many people want to go on in a monolithic way, but I believe we are pluralists, we are diverse, and this diversity has come from the different regions of Latin America, and enriches us. Some think the movement has solidified, but I'm confident the adolescent is still running.

What future do you see for Chile?

This depends on the will of the politicians. The only way to get rid of Pinochet is with a common front – from the democratic Right all the way to the Communists without excluding anyone – because Pinochet's dominance and control are so strong. The only real alternative is for people to unite to vote No in the plebiscite. This is the only way to show the US we want democracy, and to tell them this man has to leave our government. But it has to be a vigorous and open movement; nobody should make a political pact trying to negate others. Either there is unity or there is Pinochet. Whoever claims otherwise, no matter how many nuances he adds, is lying. Pinochet or unity. I am ready to enter an alliance with anyone to finish with Pinochet.

Two Types of Censorship

Andrzej Wajda

Everyone knows that there are two types of censorship. There is internal censorship which the artist imposes on himself motivated by his fear of the unknown. Then there is external censorship which is exercised under constraint by various institutions called upon to maintain that which is known as order, morality, etc.

Only too often one speaks of censorship only in connection with restrictions imposed on artists by the state, especially if that state finances artistic production and if the artists, so to speak, are only working for money. This is a simplification. Real censorship is motivated by fear about going beyond the prevailing ideas of decency, taste and even social or moral prejudices. When I was young I used to watch *Les Amants* by Louis Malle with breathtaking fascination. To me the film embodied an unrestrained erotic freedom. Much later, *The Empire of the Senses* by Oshima taught me that this sphere has no boundaries. I have often had to give interviews to foreign journalists, explaining how political censorship worked in Poland. None of them was ever able to explain to me why no films had ever been made in France – where there is no political censorship – on subjects as fraught with social and political consequences as the war in Algeria or May 1968. Does internal censorship take the place of political censorship?

Here is an extract from a confidential document of Polish censorship:

II. Circular   Warsaw, 16 July, 19-
No. ZI-Pf-132/18/75   Confidential
                                    Copy No. 24

Information from Censor No.18

I am sending the censorship units the text of 'some remarks in connection with the discussion of A. Wajda's film *The Promised*

Land', prepared by the Ideological Action Department at the Central Committee of the Polish United Workers' Party.

The Director (Julian Pelczarski)

A. Wadja is one of the four directors of the Polish cinema who have attained a high reputation throughout the world. He is one of the two (the other is Zanussi) who work in Poland. His film work is stagey; moreover, the interviews he has given reveal that he lacks an ideological and political commitment in our favour. Instead, he has adopted a position which one encounters frequently among artists – that of an 'objective judge' of past and present history – reckoning that he has the right and objective possibilities to apply standards of humanism and ethics to all worldwide problems without having recourse to Marxism or any other philosophical or social system.

The cinema is an art that speaks to the masses. It interests all who seek to lead the masses. By force of circumstance the film-maker is placed between the public to whom he would like to convey his feelings – and the regime. There are no doubt fortunate countries where this principle does not apply. But more often than not one is so bored there that even the most disturbing cry from deep within the soul is of no consequence.

Shakespeare's play *Richard III* presents the king in an unfavourable light, to say the least.

From the point of view of certain historical facts the character of Richard can also be interpreted quite differently. In England there has long been a group whose objective is to restore the lost honour of Richard III. True, this group has not achieved very much. It is difficult to change an established image projected by Shakespeare's 'politically unjust' play, simply by using arguments which may be correct but which have no myth to act as a vehicle.

This is exactly what the regime fears: that the artist may make judgments off the top of his head without taking into account the laws of history or the dilemmas of the regime or even 'exceptionally complex' political circumstances. In its determination to avoid all this the socialist state finances artistic production in its entirety – from literature to the cinema.

By financing it, the state controls it. That is why the artist, and more particularly the film director in these countries, is a personality full of contradictions, at times even a magical one.

While making my films over the years I have had to submit to censorship: I cut out scenes, above all bits of dialogue, because for the censor the preferred channel of ideology is the word. Fortunately, the cinema is the image, or to be more exact, that intangible 'something' between sound and picture which is the soul of film. Of course one can cut this or that word in *Ashes and Diamonds,* but one cannot censor the actions of Zbyszek Cybulski. It was precisely the way he behaved that represented that 'something' which was a political obscenity at the time: the freedom of the boy wearing black spectacles in the face of an imposed reality. The same applied to *Man of Marble.* The film was totally inadmissible: what could scissors have changed?

The crucial problem of political cinema is not to accept or reject interference by the censor but to create work that makes the censor's methods inoperable! Only what stays within range of the censor's imagination can be censored. Create something really original and the censors will throw away all their scissors and mumbo jumbo.

Screening Disaster

Karen Rosenberg

Documentaries have been among the first film genres to react to the massive changes sweeping Soviet society because, like magazine and newspaper articles, they can be produced and brought to the public quickly. For many years, the non-fiction film was in decline in the USSR, compromised by its subservience to the reigning ideology, and failed to attract many talented directors. With glasnost, it is gaining not just attention but respect. Lawrence Sapadin, executive director of the New York-based Association of Independent Video and Film-makers, noted the audience's excitement at the first international non-feature film festival held in Leningrad in January. 'There was a collective release,' he said, 'at seeing up on screen things that had long been swept under the rug.'

But a Ukrainian documentary that was shown out of competition in Leningrad has been withdrawn from circulation. Entitled *Threshold*, it is a 1988 work by Rolan Sergienko about the health effects of the accident at the Chernobyl nuclear plant. Before perestroika, the responsibility for banning films lay primarily with Goskino, the Soviet film agency. But in late December 1986, the conservative head of Goskino, Filip Yermash, was replaced by the more liberal Aleksandr Kamshalov. And, in fact, the shelving of *Threshold* cannot be blamed on Goskino.

Ukrainian film-maker Yuri Ilyenko, in the US at the end of March, clarified that the powerful forces behind the ban are the Ministries of Public Health, of Defence, and of Energy and Electrification. They are accusing the film of exhibiting an emotional bias and distorting facts.

Apparently, the most controversial scenes are those in which seriously ill people, who lived or worked in the Chernobyl area at the time of the accident, are interviewed in hospital. The diagnoses on their medical charts indicate that they are suffering from the most ordinary ailments, not radiation-related conditions. From this description, it is clear that *Threshold* concerns more than Chernobyl; it documents the continuation of old methods of hiding and doctoring data.

Those methods have also been visible in some other Soviet films about the nuclear disaster. In *Chernobyl: Chronicle of Difficult Weeks* (1986) by the late Vladimir Shevchenko, the old-fashioned male narrator with a voice of authority states that the man who heads a team charged with restoring the soil around Chernobyl to agricultural use is a state prize-winner. But all the prizes in the world can't bridge the credibility gap in this film. In it, the withholding of information after the accident and the lack of planning are covered up by paeans to the heroism of emergency workers.

Rolan Sergienko's previous film, *The Bells of Chernobyl* (1986), made with Vladimir Sinelnikov, is a more honest effort. One Ukrainian woman who is interviewed asks why people were not told about the accident earlier. A physician excuses the fact that he didn't warn people to close their windows by explaining that this was not within his sphere of activity! But there is something 'wet' about the film's ending, which calls only for a better interaction of people with technology.

Judging from reports in the *Wall Street Journal*, (6 March 1989) a recent film, George Shklyarevsky's *Microphone*, is more hard-hitting. The documentary showed that agricultural products from the Chernobyl area are being processed and sold elsewhere in the USSR. And Shklyarevsky created a sensation by revealing the radiation levels in an inhabited village near the plant. After the film was released, those figures could be discussed; before then, scientific researchers who knew them were subject to strict secrecy laws.

But it is not clear how long such investigative journalism will continue. In the USSR (as in other countries) nuclear energy is emerging as an exceptional topic, in which the general level of freedom of speech does not apply. On 26 April 1989, *Izvestiya* reported that new curbs had been ordered by the Ministry of Energy and Electrification on the disclosure of information about failures and accidents at nuclear plants. In the new atmosphere inaugurated by Gorbachev, these measures are not going unchallenged, however. *Izvestiya* itself criticized the new orders, writing, 'How long will the departments interested in keeping their secrets determine the limits of glasnost?' and 'How can we get rid of the zones outside of criticism?' (*New York Times*, 27 April 1989.)

Similarly, the Soviet Film-makers Union and Kiev's Dovzhenko

Studio are reportedly arguing for the re-release of *Threshold*. In many ways, the situation in the USSR can be compared to a civil war, with (sometimes high-ranking) brothers fighting brothers. The battle over the ability to report fully on nuclear energy, in print or on film, is only one front, and it is probably too early to declare which side has won.

No Ecstasy, Please, We're British

Caspar Henderson

On 14 December 1989 the video appeals committee of the British Board of Film Classification (BBFC) upheld a decision to ban *Visions of Ecstasy* on the grounds of blasphemy. The video may now only be shown privately where no money is charged. So you may let your wives and servants see it.

The 18-minute video is based on the mystical writings of the Spanish nun of the sixteenth century, St Teresa of Avila. It includes sequences in which St Teresa is shown erotically caressing the body of Christ, and sexually embracing a female who is said by video makers to represent her alter ego.

The fact that the director employed *Penthouse* pin-up and professional stripper Louise Downie to portray St Teresa had prompted charges of sexism and greedy publicity scams. However, the highly distinguished barrister Geoffrey Robertson, QC, representing the video's makers, Axel Ltd, argued that it is a serious work which examines the relationship between female sexuality and religious mysticism. He said, too, that the BBFC was acting on pure speculation and pre-empting the right of a jury to judge the film.

Among those who make submissions to the video appeals committee were the film-maker Derek Jarman, the novelist Fay Weldon, and the writer and critic Marina Warner. Ms. Warner, an eminent scholar of the history of women and Christianity, noted: 'The concept of ravishment as divine love is central in Catholic and Protestant metaphysics of the 16th Century. *Visions of Ecstasy* interprets this legacy in cinematic terms, translating the literary imaginings (of St Teresa) into visual equivalents, directly connected to works of art, images of Christ's passion ... and to Bernini's (statue) *The Ecstasy of St Teresa* ... As a film, this stands in conscious succession to *Black Narcissus*, by the oldest living master of British cinema, Michael Powell, which has been shown on the BBC as a classic.'

Nigel Wingrove, the director of *Visions*, said he was prepared to take the case on to the Law Courts, adding 'in any other (European) country I'm sure we wouldn't face this problem'. Highly critical of the BBFC's power, he hopes the film will prompt a review of this body which came into being on a wave of 'video nasty' hysteria in 1984. After judgment John Stevenson, who produced the video, accused the BBFC of packing the appeals committee: 'In my eyes the majority of the committee were older members of the conservative establishment.' However Fay Weldon, who frequently sits on the committee, but who in this case testified in defence of the video, said: 'I have the highest regard and respect for my fellow members. We sit on a rota. It wasn't my turn.'

It looks unlikely that the case will help those who wish to see the blasphemy law in the United Kingdom strengthened and widened to include other religions besides Christianity. Geoffrey Robertson has mentioned that the Law Commission has already produced two reports recommending the abolition of the blasphemy law altogether. Fay Weldon commented: 'the law in this area isn't an ass, it's a camel, and I hope the last straw of a precedent pretty soon breaks its back. I speak metaphorically. I wouldn't want you to think I was encouraging cruelty to animals.'

Industry and Hypocrisy

Pedro Almodóvar

Translated from the Spanish by Norman Thomas di Giovanni
Published in El Pais, Madrid, *22 April 1990*

New York is a real cesspit, one of the most expensive in the world, daubed from head to toe and splattered with ruins as if it had survived a nuclear war. But in its decay it is a splendid city, full of volume that shoots off in all directions, cinematographic to the ninth degree. I adore this city.

We fans of Madrid have always found the Spanish capital quite similar to the golden New York of the 1970s. Yet the United States makes me think more and more of the Spain of the 1950s. Except for the cultural and economic differences (both enormous), there is in the air the same Kafkaesque feeling of dark intransigence that there was 30 years ago in Franco's Spain – the same fear, the same difficulty in talking about reality, the same hideous paradox, the same cruel self-censorship, and sometimes the same humour for getting round it.

In *Ishtar*, a terrible film with Warren Beatty and Dustin Hoffman in the lead, Beatty curses a small plane flying overhead with the words, 'I fuck you twice', thus damning the plane two-fold while using the word 'fuck' just once. This is because, among the inane regulations of the Motion Picture Association of America (MPAA), which is responsible for rating films for release, the word 'fuck' can be used only as a simple expletive and never with a sexual connotation, and even in this way – as an exclamation – never more than three times if the film is not to be given an R certificate, and there are films made basically for younger viewers that cannot be released with such a rating. Something similar happened to the director John Waters in his first film for Universal, one of the big studios. In *Crybaby*, his latest picture, Patty Hearst plays a cop, a circumstance that increasingly justifies the use of bad language.

Waters' film was made for a teenage public, as was *Grease*, and an R certificate could have spelt its ruin at the box office. In order to secure a PG 13 certificate for *Crybaby*, Patty Hearst's mouth had also to be silenced of an excess of 'fucks'.

According to the MPAA, verbs are the worst. Another wicked verb is 'to get laid'. I am speaking of Stephen Frears' *Sammie and Rosie Get Laid*. Frears' distributor had to drop part of the title from the adverts – the 'get laid', of course – if the newspapers were to list the film.

In the old days – that is, some 25 years ago, in the full revolutionary style of the 1960s – to be given an X certificate was considered almost an advantage; it was a chic, intellectual stigma, and along with it went the impression that with an X certificate went excommunication.

Those were the days of *Last Tango in Paris, Midnight Cowboy*, and *A Clockwork Orange*. All of these were X-rated and appreciated specifically for their excesses. Today this kind of snobbery no longer exists, and an X can mean a film's commercial death. There are newspapers that refuse to list X-rated films and cinemas that refuse to show them. Scared distributors may decide in such cases to go on release unrated with a simple warning that a particular film is strong.

In the United States everything carries a warning. The North Americans' care of their mental and physical health is obsessive. Over the bar at a rock concert an outsized poster warns pregnant rock-and-rollers that alcohol is a danger to child-bearing. Such a poster makes sense only if the pregnant women, as well as being a rock fan, is also mentally retarded. At the entrance of discotheques you are asked for two proofs of age if you want to drink. Once vetted, you are given a plastic bracelet to wear which must be shown to the waiter each time you order a beer. One night at one of these discos I was a guest, so I did not go past the bouncers. When I asked the waiter for a beer he demanded to see my little plastic bracelet. I had to go back to the cloakroom, find my passport and a credit card, show them to the bouncers in order to get a plastic bracelet, and return to the bar with the satisfaction of having fulfilled the demands of bureaucracy.

Flattering as it was at 38 to be taken for a teenager, I found the proceedings somewhat pointless. Last year, at a bar in Los Angeles, some friends and I were asked for proof of age. We thought it was a joke or that for some reason we were not welcome there, but the doormen were quite serious. 'It's the law,' they said.

It's the law. Yet, the law does not prevent the mayor of Washington from exercising his duties, which include campaigning for re-election, after he has been filmed by the FBI puffing on a pipeful of crack.

But let us get back to films. Distributors fearful of the reprisals that an X-certificate film risks can show their film unrated but with the warning 'be it on your own head'. The fact of the matter is that to release an unrated film may also prove risky because many newspapers and cinemas will have nothing to do with such pictures.

Ignoring this reality, the other day – with extreme cynicism – Jack Valenti, president or executive chief of the MPAA, confidently claimed to the *New York Times* that his rating scheme never meant censorship, but was simply a guide to prevent children from viewing strong pictures. And that the information he provided was aimed exclusively at parents. That is, that in the United States no one acts as a censor – it was only a matter of friendly guidelines.

Sheer euphemism. Things must be called by their name or else one lies. Words have their own meaning; I say words but letters have them too. G, apt for any public; PG, children must be accompanied by their parents; PG 13, very dangerous for kids under 13 even if accompanied by a parent; R, restricted – even a 17-year-old must be accompanied by an adult; and X, which means filth, beware of the director, who is some sort of criminal. Valenti's statements demonstrate the MPAA's hypocrisy, its cynicism, its abuse of authority, and its rejection of everything related to freedom of expression.

In the same *Times* article, the North American director Paul Schrader (*Blue Collar, American Gigolo, Cat People*, etc.) spoke of the MPAA's Machiavellian system of censorship, which does not cut pictures but puts the scissors in the director's hands for him to do the cutting. What would Jack Valenti call this – self-censorship or self-guidance? When a director signs with a studio, a clause in his contract stipulates that he will take pains to ensure that the film will not receive an X certificate. Depending on the product, if the picture is aimed at a young audience he jeopardizes himself with an R or a PG 13 certificate. Once the film is finished, if the MPAA considers it to contain images or sounds deserving of an X certificate, they furnish a list of the offending images or words to the studio so that the author can clean his film up. The author has no recourse but to obey, because it's there in black and white in his contract. If after the first pruning something objectionable remains, the studio takes over the mutilation, following MPAA guidelines.

Like all censorship, that exerted by the MPAA is ridiculous, irrational, hypocritical, slovenly, and self-interested. Morally aberrant films like *Conan the Barbarian, Rambo*, and *Fatal Attraction* never received X certificates. It does not matter that they are true celebrations of blood and violence or that they mask an out-and-out fascist viewpoint;

they are superproducts that the industry (and it must not be forgotten that the MPAA represents industry) is interested in upholding.

In March–April, four films that are clearly not pornographic received the fatal X: Henri, *Portrait of a Serial Killer*; *Wild Orchids*; *The Cook, the Thief* ...; and my own film, *Atame*. The showing of masterpieces by the photographer Robert Mapplethorpe is persecuted and withdrawn from where it is being put on; and ironbound control exists at the entrances of discos and in literature. One cannot speak of a wave of conservatism. The gigantic wave arrived some time ago and has settled in with full awareness. Of course, there are reactions in the newspapers and in the streets, but this does not strike me as enough, bearing in mind the enormous danger that censorship represents for all aspects of freedom.

I do not accept censorship (I must be very badly trained) and I look down on the existence of organizations like the MPAA. As regards the need for rating guidelines for the public, the system adopted by this organization is confused, limited, and slack. I understand, for example, that in the case of *Henry* – a very difficult but masterly film – the public had to be warned of its nature as a 'descent to the hell of the human soul' so that any viewer not wishing to make the journey could be informed. But it is unjust, confusing, and wrong for it to be rated like a pornographic film. Equally wrong and confusing is that *Atame* should receive the same certification as *Henry*, a film which I admire but which has features completely unlike my own film. What the media and distributors demand is a broadening of the rating system, the creation of new letters which give more specific guidance. Neither *Henry* nor *Atame* can be rated as pornographic simply because they are not.

My own life has always been a paradox, and in the United States I really find myself in my element. In spite of all the problems, *El Deseo Inc.* is at this moment negotiating the rights for the North American version of *Atame*.

The MPAA rejects the love scene between Antonio Banderas and Victoria Abril (to my surprise, it has no objection whatever to the film's violent parts, which was what I feared at the outset). I feel quite proud of this scene and I know that the actors do too. Even the film's least enthusiastic viewers have found this their favourite scene.

In the film, Victoria and Antonio are two young people on the fringes of society who have been denied almost everything. They own only their feelings and their bodies. They are in love, and in this scene they make love with joy, sincerity, and the passion which this act deserves. There is no social system that forbids two healthy young lovers from enjoying the pleasure that nature has bestowed. Luckily, nobody can take that away from them – not even Jack Valenti and his whole Motion Picture Association of America.

I hope that this annoying matter will not have too much influence in the marketing of the picture in America. But I have to dig in my heels, even if my efforts come to nothing. Luckily, my future does not depend on the United States. Fifteen years ago, I lost my fear, and I do not want to get it back even for all the money in the world. I may be the last person capable of judging my own film, but I believe that I am the best person to explain my own intentions.

Turkey: Two Steps Forward, One Back

Chris Hellier

At the Istanbul International Film Festival last April, the best Turkish Film of the Year Award went to *Blackout Nights*, by director Yusuf Kurçenli. The film examined torture and censorship in Istanbul during the 1940s, a time when the Turkish government, anxious to preserve their neutrality during World War II, persecuted anyone suspected of Communist or Fascist sympathies. Fifty years later, political limits are still being imposed on Turkish film-makers and, despite the lifting of many restrictions since Turkey's return to civilian government in 1983, there are Turkish films which cannot be shown in the country.

Restrictions on directors' freedom are enshrined in a number of controversial and much-debated articles of the Turkish Penal Code, framed under military rule in the early 1980s. Article 140 covers the dissemination of derogatory information about Turkey from abroad; articles 141 and 142 outlaw communist activities; article 163, aimed at protecting the country's secular status, proscribes religious activities seeking the establishment of a theological state. In addition, film-makers are subject to the censor's scissors, most frequently wielded on pornographic material.

Following Turkey's 1980 coup, the third in 20 years, sweeping decisions were made which banned the complete works of several directors, chief among whom was Yilmaz Güney, Turkey's best-known director, who helped to transform Turkish cinema during the 1970s.

Among other directors to have had blanket bans imposed on their works following the 1980 coup was veteran film-maker Hailit Refig, principal theoretician of the 1960s approach to the creation of a national cinema. At the time of the take-over, Refig was completing an eight-hour television serial, *The Tired Warrior*, based on a novel by Kemal Tahir, whom the government considered a Communist.

The Tired Warrior, a historical work about Turkey's Independence War prior to the proclamation of the Republic in 1923, stressed that Mustafa Kemal Ataturk, Turkey's revered first president, was not the only leader in the struggle for independence. To belittle Ataturk's role runs counter to the establishment view of history and is anathema to the Turkish military. The film was seized by the authorities before being screened; all copies were destroyed; Refig was dismissed from Turkish Radio and Television (TRT); all his work was banned from television.

After the military relinquished power in 1983, Refig's work remained black-listed for three years. His films re-appeared on television in 1986, but until then 'many producers were afraid to work with me because they were afraid of state reaction,' Refig explained in a recent interview. Although he has had no further brushes with authority *The Tired Warrior* remains a personal memory.

Refig's latest production, *Karilar Kogusu* ('The Woman's Ward'), is also based on a novel by Kemal Tahir. The film examines the author's experience of prison in the 1940s, his impressions of women detainees and the reasons for his incarceration. Tahir was convicted of influencing his brother, a non-commissioned officer, to provoke a battleship revolt, a charge which Refig maintains is false. Karilar Kogusu won Turkey's Golden Orange Award for best film in 1990 and is an indication of the extent to which censorship was relaxed in the latter half of the 1980s.

Despite an easing of restrictions, however, a number of films have recently been banned by provincial authorities often under pressure from local political groups. Ali Özgenturk's 1987 film, *Su Da Ynar* (Water also Burns), was banned because of scenes deemed 'harmful to the moral ethics of society'. The film is concerned with the problem of creation, and told through the eyes of a director struggling to make a film. It is related to the work of communist poet Nazim Hikmet who fled to the Soviet Union in the early 1950s following his release from prison. Its references to Hikmet, who, like all communists in Turkey, was considered subversive, led to the film's black-listing. The incident, Dorsay believes, is the 'only significant example of film censorship in recent years'.

In early 1988, a Turco-Swedish film-maker, Muammer Özer, had his film *Cloud In Love* confiscated from the offices of an Istanbul film company. Officially, it was seized, despite Özer's dual nationality, because he was a foreigner working in Turkey without the required permission.

But the reasons for seizure were more closely related to the film's theme than its director's status. The film, a drama about a family living through years of strained relationships and disintegration, was again based on a poem by Nazim Hikmet, and included scenes of torture under military rule. Before the film was presented to the censorship board, the police, ever sensitive to charges of custodial mistreatment, illegally confiscated the footage and held it for two months. It was subsequently released, and shown, uncut, in principal cities.

Foreign films are frequent targets for the Turkish censor. Feisty and not so feisty sex scenes in films such as Jacques Beinex's *Betty Blue* rarely escape the censor's conservative scissor. Other banned imports include the controversial *Midnight Express*. Its bluntly anti-Turkish, and largely inaccurate, portrayal of a US hashish smuggler's treatment in a Turkish prison made it an obvious target.

In 1990, the Turkish government bowed to the pressure of neighbouring Iran against the showing of a scene in a US film *Naked Gun*, a parody of police movies. Iran, with whom Turkey has fragile and frequently strained relations, officially protested about a scene in the film which lampoons the late leader of the Iranian revolution, Ayatollah Ruhollah Khomeini. At the beginning of the film the revered Islamic leader, plotting to bring down the US government, is punched by a US agent who knocks off his turban to display an orange punk hair-cut. Edited versions of the film were screened in Turkey, although Istanbul's Atlas cinema refused to cut the offending scene and was closed by the city's Security Directorate.

Turkish TV producers work under similar constraints to film-makers. The country's broadcasting laws decree that Turkish television 'must conform to the state's national security, political and economic interests and should observe the ethics and values of Turkish traditions and morals'. Under the 1982 Constitution, only the state can own and operate television stations, although there are signs that TRT monopoly status may be about to change.

Tight government control prevents the dissemination of influences considered undesirable: communism, Islamic fundamentalism and Kurdish rights all come under this rubric. Further restrictions on reporting or producing documentaries about Turkey's troubled south-east, where Kurdish activists have been fighting a guerrilla war against the Turkish army since 1984, were imposed last April. Coverage of regional events by state television is now allowed only in consultation with the Interior Ministry and the National Security Council.

Self-censorship has become a problem in the Turkish media, particularly in television, the most influential medium in a country of

57 million people where newspaper circulation is less than four million copies daily.

It is practised by film-makers as well as their TV counterparts. It happens well before productions confront the hurdle of the censorship board. Foreign films for TV are subjected to particularly careful scrutiny. Sex, pornography, slang and swear words are the main targets, although many apparently innocuous foreign productions have failed to pass the Turkish censor's concept of right and wrong. In the early 1980s, *Little House on the Prairie* was taken off the air as 'religious propaganda', while a *Dynasty* series was refused by TRT's selection committee because of its portrayal of a homosexual character.

More recently, in July 1989, half way through the screening of a 1951 French film *Les Jeux Interdits* (Forbidden Games) by director René Clément, the screen went blank. TRT officials explained that the programme was taken off the air because several viewers had telephoned complaining that the film contained 'Christian propaganda'. The story revolved around a young boy and girl collecting crosses from churches and graveyards during World War II. Conservative Islamic circles subsequently thanked TRT's director for the decision; liberal and progressive opinion denounced the incident as a broadcasting scandal.

The *Forbidden Games* controversy is symptomatic of Turkey's deep-rooted religious sensitivities and growing Islamic influence. During the 1980s, TRT became a tool of the struggle between secularist liberals and the conservative Islamic lobby. There are accusations that TRT is being increasingly used for party political purposes, devoting a disproportionate amount of air time to President Turgat Özal and the policies of his ruling ANAP (*Motherland*) Party.

Discussion on human rights issues by state television, even within the limits of the law and despite wide coverage in national newspapers, has also been curtailed recently. Last September, a two-part documentary, *The Changing World and Turkey* was cut from just over an hour to 34 minutes. The deleted half hour covered the views of academics, journalists and statesmen on human rights in Turkey and included discussion of articles 141, 142 and 163 of the Penal Code.

Top politicians, including President Turgat Özal, frequently hint that changes to the Code can be expected at some undefined future date, legitimizing, for instance open discussion of communism. But while the more serious papers continue to discuss the restrictive articles, current proposals to amend the constitution may allow the establishment of private television companies. Sedat Örsel, deputy head of TRT, believes that one or two private stations may begin broadcasting in 1991. If so, the companies involved would be subject to similar restrictions and their programming schedule subject to the consent of the supreme watchdog committee on television.

The question of private television in Turkey came up last summer when the first Turkish independent station, Magic Box, began transmissions via satellite from West Germany. Although Magic Box has challenged TRT's broadcasting monopoly, it has no intention of competing with a broader coverage of events than is allowed by Turkey's broadcasting laws.

Since full transmissions began last September, Magic Box viewers have been offered a middle-of-the-road diet of league football, quiz shows and games. For those willing to pay, party political broadcasts add to the menu, but investigative political and social documentaries are against company philosophy. According to Tunça Toskay, Magic Box's chairman and a former head of TRT, touchy human rights issues, including torture, workers' rights and the aspirations of ethnic minorities, are being avoided – voluntarily.

Hope deferred

Turkey's veteran film-maker, Yilmaz Güney, (1937–84) a socialist who sympathized with the Kurdish cause, was imprisoned for 'communist propaganda' in 1961. Yet far from being political tracts, his films were realistic studies of the lives of the peasantry and working class from the poorer regions of Anatolia. His work is in the mould of the post-war neo-realism of Italy, or the later work of France's *cinema verité*.

Güney's own background enabled him to represent village life more accurately than any previous director. In 1974 Güney, given to outbursts of violence, killed a local judge during an argument in a casino and was sentenced to eighteen years' imprisonment for murder.

After serving seven years, he escaped, fled to Europe and went into hiding in France. The military regime stripped Güney of his citizenship for refusing to return to Turkey and for discrediting the country from abroad through his films. All of these, along with his books and writings, were banned.

The decree which prohibits the presence and distribution of works of art by those promoting 'anti-Turkish propaganda' is still in force, but there are signs that the decree used to ostracize Güney may no longer be lawfully applicable. After a decade of imposed silence, one of Güney's earlier films, *Umut* (Hope), was screened in Turkey at the beginning of 1990.

Umut, an important film in the history of Turkish cinema, was a turning point for Güney. It tells the story of Cabbar, a simple cart driver, played by Güney himself who, in an effort to strike it rich, squanders his pathetic wage on lottery tickets. When his horse, Cabbar's sole means of livelihood, is killed by a car, he seeks legal redress. But compensation is refused by the authorities following intervention by the well-heeled car driver. In an effort to survive, Cabbar goes in hopeless quest of buried treasure, supposedly hidden beneath a gnarled old tree.

Umut only returned to Turkey through the efforts of the leftist and pro-Kurdish weekly *Towards 2000*, a publication which was forced to cease publication last summer after the imposition of reporting restriction from the south-eastern Kurdish areas and the unwillingness of printers to accept contracts for the magazine.

Once Güney had been stripped of his citizenship, his films were considered foreign imports and, like all imported films, had to be passed by a culture committee before they could be shown in Turkish cinemas. *Towards 2000* staffers attempted to import the film for presentation to the committee but were blocked by the Ministry of Culture who refused customs clearance. Lawyers acting for *Towards 2000* argued that Güney, who died of cancer in 1984, could no longer produce 'anti-Turkish propaganda from abroad' and consequently his works should not be banned. An appeal to the Supreme Administrative Court was successful: the court removed the ministry's prohibition on *Umut* and the preview committee gave the go-ahead.

The successful screening of *Umut* raised hopes that restrictions on other Güney films might be lifted. Former *Towards 2000* journalists plan to challenge the bans on such films as *Arkadas* ('The Friend') and *Yol* ('The Path'). The latter, generally regarded as Güney's best film, is an epic story of a country undergoing rapid change told through the experience of five prisoners returning home during a prison furlough. It was the co-recipient of the Cannes Golden Palm award in 1982.

Restrictions on Güney's films have more to do with his leftists politics, his flight from prison and his anti-military and pro-Kurdish proclamations while abroad, than with the films' contents. In theory, says Atilla Dorsay, cinema critic of the liberal daily *Cumhuriyet*, Güney's films are 'not really banned'. The legal situation is clouded in confusion. Further efforts to show his films should, Dorsay believes, pass the hurdle of the Administrative Court although no one wants to take the responsibility for giving definitive clearance. In an interview which discussed *Umut* soon after its unbanning, Yilmaz Güney asserted that 'the Turkish people are not aware of what the future will bring or what hope is. Our people are constantly waiting for something.'

Iran: Islamic Visions and Grand Illusions

Reza Allamehzadeh

Translated by John O'Kane

Fourteen centuries after the coming of the Prophet, the Islamic Revolution in Iran has set about putting into effect the Qu'ran's sacred command to ban the image. One of the revolutionary movement's first steps was the burning of cinemas in Tehran and other cities throughout Iran. Cinema burning reached its climax in September 1978, when the Rex Cinema in Abadan in the south of Iran was set on fire by religious fundamentalist supporters of the Imam Khomeini, who had locked all the exists of the cinema which contained an audience of over 400 people. Three hundred and seventy-seven men, women and children, who had come to watch an Iranian film were burned alive.

This was the context in which Iranian cinema welcomed the coming of the Islamic Revolution. After taking power in 1979, Imam Khomeini consented, on the recommendation of his close advisors, to watch two films by Mostafa A'ghad, the US-based Arab film director. Both these films, *The Messenger* and *Omar Mokhtar*, are specimens of Hollywood big-budget commercial productions, which deal with Islamic subjects.

In due course, Khomeini enunciated one of the obscure, oracular pronouncements which established his reputation as an unequalled master of ambiguity. 'We are not against cinema, we are against prostitution.' Since then, Iran's film industry has been trying to establish its interpretation of the Imam's word.

The extreme orthodox view maintains that the pronouncement means, 'We are against cinema because it is prostitution.' But the present trend in government institutions which regulate the film industry, interprets the statement as, 'We are against that kind of cinema which is prostitution, not against Islamic cinema.' It has taken the Islamic regime several years to realize that the notion of an Islamic cinema is an illusion.

Mohsen Tabatab'i, director of the cultural department of the biggest government institution for Islamic film production, has declared, 'The best definition of Islamic cinema is that the cinema must play its own role in propagating Islam, just like a mosque.' To achieve this goal, the film foundation is spending 200–300 million rials (US$25–40 million) every year on promoting new Islamic films. Known as the *Bonyad-e-Mostazafan* (The Foundation of the Weak), the institution owns approximately 80 per cent of Iran's cinemas. During the last five years, Iran has produced, on average, 60 full-length films a year. In Tehran alone there are more than 100 cinemas with a regular audience upwards of 2,000,000 every month. In the smaller cities and towns, the statistics show even higher rates of attendance. In a nation with 70 per cent illiteracy, cinema is the most popular form of entertainment. Its conversion as a form of Islamic propaganda is a primary goal of the present regime. In addition to the *Bonyad-e-Mostazafan*, the government has set up a dozen Islamic foundations to put into practice the theory of an Islamic cinema: these include The Artistic School of Islamic Propaganda Organisation and The Faraby Foundation. Of 57 feature films produced in 1988, only 22 were made by non-governmental film companies.

The lion's share of resources goes to films such as *War! War! Until Victory!*, a genre which attempted to attract young boys to sacrifice their lives in the Iraq–Iran War. Other films attempt to justify an Islamic philosophical outlook or the specific policies of the Islamic regime; policies such as making the veil obligatory for women and executing political opponents.

Three genres are common in mass cinema. The most original, and at times amusing, is the miraculous, so bad it's almost good. Divine intervention plays a crucial part in resolving the plot, as in Makhmalbaf's film *Two Eyes Without Sight*, which tells the tragic take of a newly-wed youth who is sent off to the front where he is killed in action. The focus shifts to the father-in-law who is well known in his village for his outstanding piety and happens to have a son who is blind from birth. He takes his blind son to Mashad – Iran's most popular shrine – and ties him to the gate of the shrine and behold where he miraculously regains his sight in compensation for the heroic death of the son-in-law.

In addition, there is a 'crime does not pay category' set in the Shah's time. Such films are an Iranian version of cops and robbers, their plots revolving around the world of crime and violence, principally heroin smuggling.

A third genre consists of dramas set against the backdrop of the Iraq–Iran War. *The Epic of Shiller Valley*, directed by Ahmed Hasani, tells the action-packed story of a revolutionary guard who at first appeared to be betraying Iran by joining members of the Democratic Party of Kurdistan to aid Iraq. While the protagonist turns out to be a hero in the end, Kurds who support the Kurdish movement for autonomy are represented as traitors to the Iranian cause. Films in all three groups overflow with propaganda messages and jingoistic attitudes; dozens have been produced.

The sterility of its Islamic cinema has forced the government to admit its failure, and to open the door to 'non-believing' directors who, until recently, had been barred from post-revolutionary film making. Three films which had been banned for several years were allowed a screening during the 7th Fadjer Film Festival, Iran's biggest annual film festival. On January 1989, as part of the 10th anniversary of the Islamic Revolution, the festival was held in Tehran.

All three films were made by film-makers who were already well-known before the revolution. Daryush Mehrdjui, the director of *The Cow* – the best-received Iranian film abroad – made his first film after the revolution in 1980: *The School We Used To Go To*. It was banned until 1989, not because it criticized the regime or the principles of the Islamic revolution – had this been the case, the film-maker would have faced a prison sentence, torture or exile – but because it was not made by one of the faithful. Two other films had the same problem: *Water, Wind, Dust*, by Amir Naderi, recently well-received internationally, and *Bashoo, The Little Stranger* by Bahram Beiza'i, also banned for some years, were rehabilitated at the Tehran festival.

But, despite abandoning its policy, the regime has not eased the complicated process of censorship. Every film must still pass through four separate phases of control:

- Script vetting
  A special commission considers every script at two stages: in synopsis form as well as in the final version. According to official statistics, out of 1,090 synopses and full scripts delivered to the commission from 1982–84, only 188, i.e. 17 per cent, passed this stage.
- Production approval
  Every producer must submit a complete list of all the members of the cast and crew who will be employed in making the film. Many actors and actresses are not allowed to work in the film industry because of their political views, while many others live in fear that they will be put on the blacklist.

- Checking the finished film

  The most controversial stage of Islamic censorship comes when the final product is screened by a viewing board. The all-powerful board has the right to do whatever it pleases with films submitted and is unaccountable for its decisions. The history of the last ten years does not tell the whole story. Corruption, bribery and personal vindictiveness have played their part.

- Quality grades and distribution controls

  All films which make it through the first three stages of censorship, must go before another commission to be given A, B, C or D quality ratings according to which they will fare well or badly during screening. Films which are lucky enough to get an A grade can be screened in a group of A class cinemas in Tehran and other cities for at least two weeks. The ticket will be more expensive and state radio and TV advertising will promote the film. D grade films are not allowed to advertise, cannot be shown in the big cities and the price of the ticket must be lower.

For the last two years, the film authorities have been trying to boost Iran's image by participating in international film festivals. In 1989, organisers of foreign film festivals were invited to Tehran on the 10th anniversary of the Islamic Revolution. Among them were the organisers of the International Film Festivals of London, Cannes, Lucarno and Istanbul, and of the Pyongyang Youth Festival. David Streiff, director of the Lucarno International Film Festival, wrote that: 'The few guests from abroad were very well received. We had the chance to go to Isfahan for one-and-a-half days and see, partly in a special screening, many new Iranian films.' Streiff responded by inviting Iran to enter films in the Lucarno festival, one of which was awarded third prize. Despite the fact that the director was in no way an Islamic film-maker and that the prize carries little if any international kudos, the Iranian film authorities played up the publicity in Iran, as they did when another Iranian film won first prize in the little-known Italian film festival, Rimini Cinema.

Despite the oppressive effects of Islamic censorship, there are still talented film-makers in Iran who have not given up the struggle to create films of genuine human and artistic value. While the Shah's regime was more successful in concealing from the international world the degree of censorship it imposed on artists and intellectuals, the Islamic regime is less concerned with maintaining a mask. Given the degree of repression and social control, it is a miracle that film-makers of integrity have survived at all. That they have, is a testimony to the irrepressible energy and rich cultural resources of the Iranians.

USSR: Stripping the Well-stocked Shelves

Julian Graffy

One of the key events in the liberalization of Soviet culture after Mikhail Gorbachev came to power was the Fifth Congress of the Union of Cinematographers of the USSR in May 1986. The conformist board of the union was replaced by a group headed by the younger directors Elem Klimov, Andrei Smirnov and Vadim Abdrashitov. One of the most influential decisions of the congress was the establishment of the 'Conflict Commission', headed by the former *Pravda* film critic, Andrei Plakhov. Its brief was 'discussing those films which for one reason or another were not released, and giving detailed recommendations to the State Cinema Committee for each of those films, asking the State Cinema Committee of the USSR and the cinema committees of the republics to bear these recommendations in mind when deciding on the release of the films under discussion'.

Plakhov had just returned from Tbilisi where he had attended a clandestine showing of Tengiz Abuladze's daring allegory of the Stalinist period, *Repentance (Pokaianie)*. The help of the Commission in securing a release for *Repentance* was a dry run for its later activities. By August 1988, the commission had seen 159 films, a list of which appeared in the last issue of the journal *Kinostsenarii* (Film Scenarios) for 1988. Several of them, such as a Konchalovskii's *Asia's Happiness* and Alov and Naumov's version of Dostoevskii's story *A Nasty Anecdote* had appeared in Jeanne Vronskaia's list of 51 suppressed Soviet films prepared for the special film issue of *Index* in August 1981. These included work by directors such as Tarkovskii, Paradzhanor, Klimov, Shukshin and Konchalovskii.

Speaking in London in December 1990, Andrei Smirnov, former first secretary of the union, put the number of films seen at 'about 250'.

Vol. 20, no. 3, 1991

According to Plakhov, the Commission first drew up a list of the films they knew of, some of them already the stuff of legend. Then film-makers began to come to them. Recently, several émigré directors of banned films have returned to the USSR to re-edit them for distribution.

Almost five years after the inauguration of the Commission, the distorted picture of their own cinematic history known to Soviet viewers is apparent. They were deprived of important works by directors of the stature of Tarkovskii, Paradzhanov, Ioseliani, Shepit'ko, Abuladze, Klimov and Konchalovskii. They were deprived of almost the entire careers of Kira Muratova, Aleksandr Askol'dov (who, after the banning of *The Commissar* in 1968 never made another film), the brilliant young feature and documentary maker Aleksandr Sokurov and key works by Aleksei German. And, as Plakhov points out, they were deprived of the work that did not get made at all.

An immediate consequence of this flood of hitherto unseen work was a reassessment of the achievements of the Soviet cinema. In a poll of twelve leading film critics published by the newspaper *Nedelia* at the end of 1987, several previously banned films made the top ten of a list of the best Soviet films of all time. The list was headed by German's picture of small town life in the 1930s, *My Friend Ivan Lapshin (Moi drug Ivan Lapshin)*, which narrowly beat *The Battleship Potemkin*.

All films have to be passed for release by the State Cinema Committee *(Goskino)*. It showed particular vigilance in suppressing evidence of deviation on ideologically sensitive subjects. The large number of historical films among those that fell foul of the Committee, including *The Commissar, Repentance*, the films of German, Tarkov-skii's *Mirror (Zerkalo)* and Klimov's *Agony* provide ample evidence of this process at work. In practice, censorship was more complex and more pervasive.

Another of the decisions of the Fifth Congress was that the Soviet cinematic press should develop a 'principled, demanding and competent film criticism and heighten its struggle against greyness in the cinema'. The leading cinema journal, *Iskusstvo kino* (Art of the Cinema) has become more lively; its ambitious and probing articles have revealed a good deal more about censorship in action. Historical films were especially vulnerable. Writing in the January 1989 issue of the journal, Elena Stishova traces the fate of *The Commissar* from its commissioning to celebrate the fiftieth anniversary of the revolution through to alarm that the film 'distorts the humanist essence of the proletarian revolution'.

In a series of articles that are opening up the history of cinema in the Brezhnev period, Valerii Fomin shows how watchfulness extended to every detail of Soviet life and behaviour in the present as much as the past. Film-makers were told that their characters drank too much or were too frivolous; that their films contained too much bad weather; that the picture they presented of life in the Soviet village was too drab. Anything that contradicted the sanitized version of Soviet life the censors wished to project was a potential cause for shelving, and Fomin provided documentary evidence of the measures film-makers took to meet these often ludicrous requirements. The film with too much bad weather in it was 'improved' by the insertion of a sunny walk in the woods.

But censorship was by no means confined to the State Cinema Committee. Any Soviet politician or institution objecting to a film's line could use the so-called 'telephone right' to intervene; officials within the studio often imposed changes before a film was even sent to the Committee, fearful of its wrath. The most lethal censorship was the self-censorship which film-makers imposed on their own ideas.

The Conflict Commission now sees its unshelving work as complete, but it continues to exist 'in case of need'. And there have been several recent examples of new films being prevented from reaching their audience. In theory, the state committee is now concerned only to protect military secrets, to stop calls for the overthrow of the Soviet state and to outlaw pornography. In practice, some films are simply not bought for release; 'telephone right' is used to stop others being shown in a particular town. This is often the fate of radical documentary makers, whose exposure of crime, ecological disaster or political machination proves too explosive for bureaucratic tastes. It has also happened to recent feature films. Dmitrii Svetozarov's 'ecological thriller' *The Hounds (Psy)* was banned from release in early 1990. Sergei Snezhkin's *An Emergency on a Regional Scale (Chp raionnogo masshtaba)*, with its savage dissection of the moral bankruptcy of local Komsomol leaders, was passed for showing but then banned in several cities. A Leningrad showing of Aleksandr Rogozhkin's *The Guard (Karaul)*, a horrifying account of bullying in the Soviet army, provoked an official demand from a local veterans' association that the film be withdrawn. The best known shelved film of the new era is Kira Muratova's *The Asthenic Syndrome (Astenicheskii sindrom)*.

Dear Mickey Mouse ...

Steven Goldman

Were a latter-day George Orwell to write of Hollywood at the close of
the millennium, he might envision the future of its film industry as the
yellow booties of Mickey Mouse forever dancing on the face of
humanity. Viewed from a distance, Hollywood is often generalized as
such a monolith – gargantuan, omnipotent, culturally omnipresent and
largely infantile. From within this El Dorado itself, the mood is quite
different, surprisingly hesitant, uncertain of itself and its future and, for
the greatest supplier of entertainment on a global scale, culturally
myopic.

I take the proposition of censorship in US film making lightly.
Indeed Mickey, the thought of a Big Bad Wolf denying your
constitutionally guaranteed right of free speech fails to induce any
appreciable onset of insomnia. There are several reasons for this.
Foremost is the thought of the film-maker who does not enjoy your
freedoms, the film-maker whose works have been censored or banned
outright, the film-maker who has been forced into exile or imprisoned
for his opinions, namely those stories which are documented elsewhere
in these pages. In this context, and with the memory of the injustices
suffered by US film-makers at the height of McCarthyism, the problems
faced by contemporary US film-makers working in the popular cinema
not only pale by comparison, they simply do not exist.

Instead, 1989 and 1990 saw continued obstacles to artistic
expression, largely attributable to self-imposed restraint for commercial reasons. Despite the popular success of film-maker Spike Lee's
She's Gotta Have It, Do the Right Thing, and, most recently, *Mo' Better
Blues,* Blacks and other minority interests remain under-represented in
mainstream cinema. The results of the artistic community's battle to
preserve National Endowment for the Arts (NEA) subsidies from state
approval of artistic content (as it applies to film making) are tenuous at

best. These developments, combined with the increased centralization of media ownership, conspire to form a bleaker picture for the new year for those working outside the Hollywood studio system.

In the Spring of 1990, Hollywood itself entered into a direct and highly publicized confrontation with civil authorities during Warner Brothers' controversial filming of Tom Wolfe's novel, *The Bonfire of the Vanities*.

Shooting on location in New York over an eight week period, the film-makers, led by director Brian De Palma, found themselves working in an atmosphere dominated by increasing local racial tensions while filming material which was, arguably, racially inflammatory. Filming took place concurrently with a Bensonhurst, Brooklyn murder trial in which a gang of five white youths were charged with the murder of a young black man who had ventured into a largely Italian-American neighbourhood. Given that he was dealing with potentially racially inflammatory material, the director lost his nerve about remaining true to a book that lashes out impartially against every racial group in New York. Myron Kovitsky, for instance, a 'thin bald hawk-nosed' Jewish judge in the Bronx who spits on blacks, is cast in the film as a do-right judge, played by Morgan Freeman, a black actor noted for dignity and *gravitas*. Mr De Palma admitted to the *New York Times*, 'I didn't want to racially polarize it. I didn't want a white judge talking morality to a basically black audience.' Not the point made by Tom Wolfe's book.

The issue raised during the production of *Bonfire of the Vanities* was not one of state censorship *per se*, however, but of the state's obligation to assist film-makers with the logistical problems of filming on location in the production of their films.

Bronx borough president Fernando Ferrer, in what was viewed as an attempt to appease the concerns of his constituency, denounced the *Bonfire* script for its depiction of the borough, reportedly described as a 'Hollywood hand job' by Mr Ferrer's press secretary. Mr Ferrer publicly considered leading a boycott of the Warner Brothers film, and requested a special disclaimer be attached to it, stressing that the film was a work of fiction while citing recent positive developments in the borough. Warner Brothers offered a standard one sentence disclaimer and, reportedly, a US$10,000 contribution to a community charity. Expressing his concern at Mr Ferrer's statements, New York mayor David M. Dinkins issued a statement on 27 April:

> Although borough president Fernando Ferrer is entitled to express his concerns regarding the portrayal of the Bronx in the upcoming

film, *The Bonfire of the Vanities*, I have conveyed to him my concern for his attempts to interfere with the project. He is an independent elected official, his remarks reflect only his own opinions and do not in any way express the official point of view of the city of New York. The city would never consider requesting a painter, author, or playwright to alter or add to an artistic creation. Film making is no different.

Following the run in between Mayor Dinkins and Mr Ferrer, the *Bonfire* crew found itself shut out of several key locations. The Metropolitan Museum of Art, The American Museum of Natural History, and a New Jersey courthouse denied Mr De Palma permission to film. According to Joseph Friedman, executive director of the New Jersey Motion Picture and Television Commission, the latter expulsion marked the first such episode in the commission's eleven year existence that a film had been denied a location because of its content.

In May, US Warner Brothers had agreed to pay the county of Essex, New Jersey, US$250,000 for permission to film for one week in the old Essex county courthouse in Newark. After learning of the court's intended depiction in the film, Judge Robert Wilentz, a chief justice of the State Supreme Court of New Jersey, denied access to the film-makers, saying the film, 'could serve to seriously undermine the confidence of black citizens in our court system'. Warner Brothers moved the scene to a second courthouse in the borough of Queens, New York at a considerably higher price, while Essex county executive Nicholas Amato, filed suit against Judge Wilentz for lost revenue. Federal Judge, Nicholas Politan, harshly criticized Judge Wilentz, ruling on 20 December that the chief justice had violated the First Amendment of the US Constitution when he banned filming. The court dismissed any financial remuneration for lost revenues in the decision and Wilentz will reportedly appeal against the decision.

The film opened on 21 December to largely negative press reviews which cited many of the concerns initially raised during the film's production.

X marks the spot

The most dramatic change affecting the regulation of motion pictures occurred in the Autumn of 1990, after a succession of legal disputes between independent film distributors and the Motion Picture Association of America, a self-regulating industry body. Following several months of controversy, the MPAA decided to drop the long established 'X' certificate, replacing it with a new rating, 'NC-17' – no children under 17 admitted. It was the first amendment of the US ratings system since 1984, when the 'PG-13' certificate was created to accommodate the film *Indiana Jones and the Temple of Doom*.

By 1990, the 'X' certificate, intended to designate a film suitable for adults only, had become synonymous with pornographic films. The change was precipitated when an increasing number of 'X' certificates were issued to non-pornographic works. The certificates severely curtailed the distribution of these films, when numerous cinemas, as a matter of policy, refused to exhibit films bearing the rating and newspapers refused to publish advertisements. Distributors, most notably Miramax Films, took issue with the MPAA in court. Miramax first filed suit with the MPAA over the British film *Scandal*. The film was eventually cut for US release when the appeal was lost. Additional court appeals were made by Miramax for films like Peter Greenaway's *The Cook The Thief His Wife and Her Lover*, Pedro Almodóvar's *Tie Me Up! Tie Me Down!* an the British thriller *Hardware*. Miramax lost all its cases in court and was subsequently called into question itself in a report published in the New York *Village Voice* which claimed that the company was 'notorious for cutting and trimming films for the American market'.

Like the controversy surrounding the NEA, it is too early to determine the overall effect of the 'NC-17' ruling, *Henry and June*, the film by Philip Kaufman based on the diaries of Anaïs Nin, was the first recipient of the new certificate. Reports of several newspapers refusing to run advertisements for the film, irrespective of the new MPAA rating, followed shortly after.

For the commercial Hollywood film-maker, it is likely that the adoption of the 'NC-17' ruling will have little liberating effect as most directors will remain contractually obliged to produce films which meet nothing stronger than an 'R' certificate. (Blockbuster Video, one of the largest chains in the US, said in January 1991 that it would not carry NC-17 films.)

In looking back at the course of recent events, it seems clear that the greatest detriment to creative expression in the US film industry remains that which is self-generated. The decision to create inoffensive films designed to reach the widest possible audiences, the exclusion of minority voices, even the classification of the films themselves, is a decision taken from within the film industry. Writers and directors working in the studio system, while still producing some of the most challenging films to be seen anywhere, publicly lament the current and continued state of affairs. As argued by US film critic Richard Corliss in his article for the September 1990 issue of *Film Comment,* the most important analysis written on the subject that year, the creators of these works must take a public stand if they are to effect any appreciable change. The Directors' Guild of America, acting in firm solidarity, could refuse contractual obligations restricting the content of their films to meet MPAA requirements. Equally, the Writers' Guild of America could push for similar contractual changes to protect their members' screenplays. Such changes would seem unlikely in the present climate, but if these artists, as a group, routinely sign away their creative control over their projects in return for financial remuneration, it is difficult to muster sympathy for their objections to a situation in which they are a partner.

No End in Sight

Philip French

When the noted UK film critic and scourge of the censors, Alexander Walker, heard that James Ferman, director of the British Board of Film Classification (as the British Board of Film Censors was renamed in 1985), was a member of the committee appointed to celebrate the centenary of cinema, he wrote a letter of protest to the committee's chariman. The reply he received referred to Ferman's probity, his devotion to the cinema and the obvious discourtesy that would be involved in seeking his resignation. A more robust response would have been to say that since its earliest days the movie industry has been in an unholy (though some would say a holy) alliance with the censors, that censorship had shaped the course of movie history and played a part in determining the language of popular cinema. It would thus be as unrealistic and disingenuous to refuse the censor a seat at the centennial feast as it would have been, 40 years ago, to deny the public hangman an invitation to a celebration of British penology.

Even before the first films were projected for a paying audience by the Lumière brothers in December 1895, the police had been intervening in Europe and North America to prevent peep-show machines from showing such innocently erotic items as *Dorolita's Passion Dance*, which was withdrawn in 1894 from the Kinetoscope Arcade on Atlantic City's Boardwalk. Whether there really was a sequence of flicker-cards or a few dozen feet of film called *What The Butler Saw* is, I believe, uncertain. But the title has entered the language and for good reason. It suggests three things – voyeurism, class and dangerously illicit activities observed and revealed to an outsider.

In 1896, one year after the Lumière show in Paris, 50 feet of film recording a gentle kiss between May Irwin and John C Rice, both middle-aged, from the Broadway play *The Widow Jones*, had US newspapers calling for it to be banned. The following year the moral opprobrium focused on screen violence as exemplified in a string of films bringing championship boxing matches to the general public. Terry Ramsaye, who lived through the period, wrote in the first comprehensive history of American cinema, *A Million and One Nights* (1926):

> One marked effect of the Corbett-Fitzsimmons picture as the outstanding screen production of its day was to bring the odium of pugilism upon the screen all across Puritan America. Until that picture appeared the social status of the screen had been uncertain. It now became definitely lowbrow, an entertainment for the great unwashed commonalty. This likewise made it a mark for uplifters, moralists, reformers and legislators in a degree which would never have obtained if the screen had by specialization reached higher social strata.

Shortly after the turn of the century, a Chicago judge claimed that the cinema was among the chief influencers – bad, of course – on the juvenile offenders who appeared before him. His sentiments were echoed over 90 years later when the English judge in the James Bulger murder trial suggested that the juvenile killers had been influenced by the American horror movie *Child's Play 3*, though the local police could find no evidence that the children had seen it.

What was it that the benign American inventor, Thomas Edison, and his French friends, the photographic manufacturers Louis and Auguste Lumière, had unleashed upon the world, and that had so rapidly led to a demand for its control? The cinema developed during a period of unprecedent social change, and broadly speaking there were seven aspects that made it seem a threatening phenomenon (to which 30 years later was added that of rebarbative language and disturbing sound).

First, there was the very size of the image and the immediacy, the intimacy of the experience. Second, film opened up life socially, geographically, in time and space, transporting audiences to places unknown, hitherto forbidden, invented. Third, the violence and eroticism were palpable, yet they left the audience unscathed. Fourth, the cinema offered an inviation to fantasize, to dream, to revolt, and it is hardly surprising that the Futurists and the Surrealists were among the first to recognize its power. Fifth, the movies rapidly became the most popular leisure activity of the burgeoning urban working classes, feared by the bourgeoisie as a potential source of revolution and by intellectual devotees of eugenics as a threat to the future of Western Civilization. Sixth, movie-going was a public activity that took place in the dark, offering terrible temptations to innocent boys and girls. Seventh, there were health and safety fears, some real, some imaginary:

fear of fire hazards from unsafe buildings and highly imflammable
nitrate film; fear that the flickering images might damage eyesight or
induce epilepsy; fear that these hot, fetid auditoriums could spread
contagious diseases.

Some early opponents of cinema wanted to crush the new medium
in the bud. In 1986, Herbert Stone, the eloquent editor of the Chicago
literary magazine, *The Chap Book*, wrote: 'I want to smash to
Vitascope. The name of the thing is itself a horror. Its manifestations
are worse.' Of the notorious Edison clip, universally known as *The
Kiss*, Stone fumed:

> When only life size it was pronounced beastly. But that was nothing
> to the present sight. Magnified to Gargantuan proportions and
> repeated three times over it is absolutely disgusting. All delicacy or
> remnant of charm seems gone from Miss Irwin, and the
> performance comes near to being indecent in its emphasised
> vulgarity. Such things call for police interference.

Wherever films were made or shown, censorship boards sprang up.
Around 1914, American producers united to oppose officially
constituted bodies, and the federal government refused to establish
film censorship at a national level, though this was precisely what
happened in virtually every other country. But a major blow was
administered in a crucial judgment by the US Supreme Court in 1915.
Delivering the majority opinion following an appeal by the Mutual
Film Corporation against censorship boards in Missouri and Ohio,
Justice McKenna stated:

> It cannot be put out of view that the exhibition of moving pictures is
> a business pure and simple, originated and conducted for profit,
> like other spectacles, not to be regarded, nor intended to be
> regarded by the Ohio constitution, we think, as part of the press of
> the country or as organs of public opinion. They are mere
> representations of events, of ideas and sentiments published and
> known, vivid, useful and entertaining no doubt, but as we have said,
> capable of evil, having power for it, the greater because of their
> attractiveness and manner of exhibition.

This decision, denying the cinema the constitutional protection
enjoyed by other media, was eventually reversed in 1952. But it set the
tone for the way the movies were to be perceived for decades, at least
in the Anglo-Saxon world, and continues to do so into the 1990s.

*

Meanwhile, in the UK, censorship came in through the back door. The 1909 Cinematograph Act was introduced to license cinemas for safety purposes and was extended by the courts to cover the movies shown in them. This led to the creation in 1912 of the British Board of Film Censors, initiated by the Home Office but run as a self-regulating body by the film industry, to license movies for public exhibition. Its second president, the ubiquitous T.P. O'Connor, Conservative MP, author and newspaper editor, served from 1916 until his death in 1929. During his reign, he made the film industry the acquiescent creature of the political establishment, a position from which it has yet to emerge.

Shortly after his appointment, O'Connor told a Cinema Committee of Inquiry that 'there are 43 rules, and they cover pretty well all the grounds you can think of'. T.P.'s rules, all of them prohibitions, prevented the production or exhibition of pictures involving 'unnecessary exhibition of underclothing', 'relations of Capital and Labour', 'realistic horrors of warfare', 'executions' and 'subjects dealing with India in which British officers are seen in an odious light'. We must remember that Britain was at war when O'Connor devised this list, but most of the rules remained in force for the next 40–50 years. Alfred Hitchcock turned away from political film-making forever when his plans to make a picture about the 1926 General Strike were rejected by the BBFC.

It was some time before the US industry produced anything as detailed as T.P.'s 43 Rules. But when it came, the Production Code was the most elaborate ever drawn up, and sought to make American movies acceptable and inoffensive to juvenile audiences at home and throughout the world. After World War I, during which US cinema began to establish the worldwide ascendancy that today seems unassailable, the Hollywood studios were coming under attack. Their films and the behaviour of their stars were agents of a changing post-war morality that small-town America found threatening. Anti-Semitism was part of this paranoia, directed towards a new industry largely created and owned by Jewish immigrants fleeing pogroms in Europe. In 1920, newspapers across the country carried an item with a Washington DC dateline that began: 'The lobby of the International Reform Bureau, Dr Wilbur Crafts presiding, voted tonight to rescue the motion pictures from the hands of the Devil and 500 un-Christian Jews.'

The response of the Hollywood moguls was to invite Will H. Hays, a middle-western Presbyterian elder and postmaster-general in Republican President Warren Harding's cabinet, to become president of the newly-constituted Motion Picture Producers of America Inc.

The year was 1921, his job to put the industry in order to preserve its leaders' fortunes. He served them well for 43 years, and the present, only the fourth, person to hold this post is another recruit from Washington, President Lyndon Johnson's right-hand man, Jack Valenti, who became MPPA president in 1966.

Hays believed in the 'Ten Commandments, self-discipline, faith in time of trouble, worship, the Bible and the Golden Rule', and at one of his first Hollywood press conferences he declared:

> This industry must have towards that sacred thing, the mind of a child, towards that clean, virgin thing, that unmarked slate, the same responsibility, the same care about the impressions made upon it, that the best clergyman or the most inspired teacher would have.

He first introduced a system by which the studios were to submit to the Hays Office the books, scripts and stories they were considering for filming. Subsequently he sent out an informal list of what he called 'Don'ts and Be-Carefuls'. The coming of sound with its possibilities for new verbal offence, along with the influx of irreverent new writers, many of them tough ex-journalists from big city newspapers, led to the adoption in 1930 of a Production Code drawn up by two midwestern Catholics, one a Jesuit professor of drama, the other a publisher of trade magazines. This Hays Office Code, made mandatory in 1934, began with three general principles – 'no picture shall be produced that will lower moral standards'; 'correct standards of life, subject only to the requirements of drama and entertainment, shall be presented'; 'law, natural or human, shall be be ridiculed, nor shall sympathy be created for its violation.' This was followed by eight double-column pages of detailed applications, ranging from the demand that 'no film may throw ridicule on any religious faith' to various proscribed words, including '*Fairy* (in a vulgar sense)'. The Code was designed to make every film suitable for audiences of any age, and remained in force until 1967 when it was replaced by a system of certificated categories. This change was influenced both by European systems of censorship, and also by European films which, with their greater freedom in the handling of sexual matters, were making serious inroads in the American market.

The Code helped shape the language of Hollywood movies and the cinema worldwide, as writers and directors argued and bargained with the Code's administrators, and invented stratagems to approach forbidden subjects and metaphors to express proscribed acts. Fireworks and crashing waves stood in for sex. Body language could suggest the taboo subject of homosexuality. A woman with shiny lipstick, or chewing gum, or smoking in the streets, was identified as a prostitute. And the public came to take with a pinch of salt the come-uppance that the Code insisted be visited on glamorous villains. Yet there were whole areas of life that were ignored and distorted.

The industry was only opposed to external censorship. It was the major studios themselves who, through their control of production, distribution and exhibition, decided who would make films and whose pictures would be distributed. When Hollywood bowed to the House Un-American Activities Commitee (HUAC) and other McCarthyite witch-hunters in the post-World War II years, a group of blacklisted film-makers produced *Salt of the Earth* (1953), an independent film about a miners' strike in New Mexico. They were harassed while on location by local and federal authorities, the leading actress was deported to her native Mexico, and the completed film was denied exhibition in the USA until the 1960s when it became a cult work among student radicals.

While this supposedly voluntary censorship was imposed in the USA, the movie-makers in the newly created Soviet Union were similarly having their talents harnessed to the cause of ideology. During the 1920s, artists were permitted considerable leeway to innovate and Pudovkin, Eisenstein and Dziga Vertov created a cinema that was revolutionary both politically and aesthetically. But with the coming of sound and the replacement of the enlightened Anatoly Lunacharsky by the philistine Stalinist cultural commissar, Andrei Zhdanov, Soviet cinema became rigidly controlled by bureaucrats and the doctrine of socialist realism strenuously imposed on the nation's artists.

Come the 1930s, and the German cinema, formerly among the least circumscribed, was taken over by the Nazis, though relatively few feature films were vehicles for explicit political propaganda. The European dictators of both left and right – Lenin and Stalin, Hitler and Mussolini – were fascinated by the cinema and aware of its power. They therefore sought to exploit it in their own interests. Artists working under them, including French film-makers of the Occupation and Eastern European cineastes of the post-war decades, could subvert censorship and censure by resorting to allegory, making movies with mythical subjects or putting them in historical settings. Likewise in Hollywood in the 1950s, when the studios were reluctant to make political films or touch on matters of race, these issues were dealt with in the guise of westerns or science fiction.

As the first great mass medium, the cinema provided the politicians and guardians of morality with the paradigm for censorship in the twentieth century. And, paradoxically in an era that has seen the democratic urge become central to social progress, there has grown up a culture of censorship, an expectation and acceptance of it. The least censorship – of films, as well as of the other arts and media – is usually found in confidently democratic countries that have recently experienced authoritarian regimes of the left or the right: in Greece and Spain, for instance, or Hungary and the Czech Republic, there is virtually no censorship of movies. But in countries that have not been exposed to such draconian treatment at the hands of the state, movies are subjected to pre-censorship that goes far beyond the methods of certification used to protect children. In Britain, for instance, where the Lord Chamberlain's role in licensing plays was abolished in 1968 and prosecutions of literary works are a thing of the past, the BBFC extends its influence and introduces new criteria. It is true that the situation has become increasingly permissive (despite a lurching, three steps forward, two steps back method of advance). But fashionable feminist sensitivities, about possible offences against women, for example, now affect the censors' judgements, and the BBFC's statutory powers to license video cassettes for home use has led to films for domestic viewing being subjected to an elaborate set of rules based on prurient and class-based assumptions about the way people (ie, the proletariat) see and perceive films.

The simple fact is that at every societal level we have been inculcated with the idea that censorship is necessary – to preserve society, to protect people from each other, to save ourselves from our baser instincts. Revolution, personal violence and sex forever lurk to disturb the status quo. And censorship is most evident in the cinema because, unlike books, plays, exhibitions, TV programmes and the radio, every film we see, every video we buy, is prefaced on the screen or on the cassette box by a certificate stating that the work has been examined (the British certificates are signed jointly by the Queen's cousin and the American-born James Ferman) and judged fit for us to see. It isn't in the interest of the film companies to reveal what the censor has excised for cinematic exhibition or video release.

One might suppose that there was enough official supervision. Sadly, the press, both popular and elitist, tabloid and broadsheet, are among the first to demand tighter control of the movies. Especially when it claims some gruesome murder has been influenced by a recent film. This isn't confined to editorial writers and sensational columnists. All too often movie critics demand that works that have offended them be cut or banned. The late Dilys Powell, the liberal critic of *The Sunday Times* from 1939 to 1975, gave evidence for the defence when

D. H. Lawrence's *Lady Chatterley's Lover* was prosecuted for obscenity in 1960. Yet she claimed in 1948 that the innocuous gangster movie, *No Orchids for Miss Blandish*, should have been given 'a new certificate of D for Disgusting'. In 1954 she supported the BBFC's total ban on the Marlon Brando biker movie *The Wild One*: 'I am bound to say I think the Board was absolutely right.'

Recently we've experienced a new form of censorship as several critics employed by British national daily newspapers have called upon the minister for national heritage to investigate the financing from public funds in Britain and Europe or movies they disapprove of, either on moral or aesthetic grounds (i.e., too arty or too sleazy). The films at issue are Michael Winterbottom's harsh road movie, *Butterfly Kiss*, and Mario Brenta's contemplative Italian picture, *Barnabo of the Mountains*.

Looking back over a century of movie censorship, like Beaumarchais' Figaro, one laughs for fear that one might cry at the fatuity and foolishness of it all. For 100 years, audiences have been treated like untrustworthy children, artists as enemies of society. The BBFC refusing a certificate for over 30 years to Eisenstein's *Battleship Potemkin* in case it should ferment mutiny in the Royal Navy. The same board, at the height of World War II holding up the distribution of *Western Approaches*, a documentary tribute to the Merchant Navy, because some torpedoed sailors in mid-Atlantic use the word 'bloody'. The French censors banning Stanley Kubrick's *Paths of Glory* in 1958 because it casts aspersions on the conduct of French officers in World War I, and Madame De Gaulle, 10 years later, attempting to have a film version of Diderot's *La Réligieuse* banned because it presented the eighteenth century Catholic Church in an unfavourable light. The Prince of Wales using his opening speech at the Museum of the Moving Image not to celebrate the cinema but to call for the banning of horror films on cassette – the so-called 'video nasties' – to protect his vulnerable children, and getting applauded by the audience of newspapermen. The Soviet authorities, unable to make any sense of Andrei Tarkovsky's autobiographical film *Mirror*, banishing it to the cinema circuit that served military bases. The New Zealand censors approving the Joseph Stick version of James Joyce's *Ulysses* only for exhibition to single-sex audiences. John Huston getting the word 'gunsel', a rare word (possibly of Yiddish origin) for catamite used by Dashiell Hammett in *The Maltese Falcon*, past the Hays Office censor, who thought it was underworld slang for a gun-toting gangster, which indeed it became after the film was released. One could go on forever, as indeed film censorship threatens to do.

Screening Rape

Jane Mills

There is a gap at the heart of mainstream portrayals of male sexual violence to women – a silence

Ambivalence is a particularly painful form of dis-ease for an ageing 1968-er. My anti-censorship credentials were once impeccable. As an officer of a national anti-censorship society, I believed the right to see violent, erotic Japanese movies was a basic human right akin to that of full employment. Pornography was a bit more complex: you could be for it (liberal humanist) or against it (humourless feminist), but mostly it was part of the argument for female sexual empowerment.

Something changed. In 1990 I made a BBC documentary, *Rape: That's Entertainment?*, to explore the cinematic representation of male sexual violence towards women in Hollywood movies. The research involved viewing over 250 movies in which women were tortured, punished and inevitably silenced.

Old habits die hard. I would wake up possessed by strong anti-censorship certainty. By teatime my liberalism was in tatters: knee-capping, frankly, seemed too good for those who skilfully, and often lovingly, produced all these degrading, demeaning and dehumanizing expressions of gynephobic phallocentricity. Ambivalence had arrived, I had to quit.

When contemplating living in Australia it was exciting to imagine a country where, unlike the UK, I was free to hire a video of *Reservoir Dogs*, where freedom of information was enshrined in law and whose classification laws state 'adults should be able to read, hear and see what they want'.

Within two weeks of arriving I was protesting the banning of the Spanish film *In A Glass Cage* from the Sydney Gay and Lesbian Film Festival. The chief censor overturned federal government legal rubric previously thought to exempt film festivals from legislation. I felt the old anger at having to discuss censorship and free speech rather than the much more important issues raided by the film – rape, child sexual abuse and the renaissance of European facism.

Australian adults face even more censorship laws: pay-TV viewers will be denied movies restricted to those over the age of 18; and the principle of free speech is about to be further qualified by 'the need to take acocunt of community concerns about ... the portrayal of persons in a demeaning manner'. Similar legislation has already been introduced in New Zealand where 'demeaning' is further emphasized with the words 'degrading' and 'dehumanizing'.

This wording is open to diverse interpretation. Casuists will doubtless delight in argument about whether the Munchkins in *The Wizard of Oz* represent the degradation of short people. Anti-censors gloomily predict the banning of classics such as *King Kong* and Australia's very own milestone film, *Jedda*, both of which have utterly demeaning portrayals of black peoples. And whose liberalism would not be tested by a show trial of Aldrich's *The Killing of Sister George*, which is devoid of a single frame of female sexual empowerment? But none of these are likely to be denied (re)classification.

Nor are the myriad mainstream movies with graphic representations of rape that indubitably will be produced in the years to come, although some might be subjected to the old snip. While I have never been persuaded of any causal connection between filmic representation and human behaviour, there is something about the way popular culture is so wedded to representations of rape that gives me a bad case of the ambivalences. I think it's because of the way the audience is invited, often successfully, to collude in a sense of it never really having happened.

This, of course, is a device that reinforces powerful cultural myths, based on men's fantasies about female sexuality that maintain no rape ever happens. As, for instance, in the notion of woman saying 'no' when she really means 'yes'. Or that she secretly desires rough sex. Or that her behaviour means she deserves it. Then there's the rapist as 'mad beast' myth – neatly placing the rapist outside the ambit of human law. Central to the myths and an analysis of the filmic representations lies a gap, an elision, a silencing. It is, of course, the female voice, the feminine perspective that is silenced, missing.

An elision also lies at the heart of the new Australian censorship legislation. The word 'rape' is not actually mentioned, but the close connections between the female experience of rape and the various denotations and connotations of the words 'demeaning', 'degrading' and 'dehumanizing' make for interesting analysis. All three words can be seen as part of a male displacement strategy rendering mute the female voice with her own definition of rape.

'Demeaning' means 'to lower in status or reputation' – a notion endorsed by laws that 'protect' a woman from public disgrace by banning publication of her name. 'Degrading' connotes 'impairment with respect to some physical property', suggesting a woman's chastity represents her commercial value and that a woman herself is little more than male property (when 'rape' entered English in the early fifteenth century, it denoted the violent seizure of goods or property). Degrading also connotes 'decomposition', offering a reminder of the guilt many abused and raped women feel – when treated like shit you can feel you are shit. 'Dehumanize' conjures up two male rape films: Boorman's *Deliverance* and Tarantino's *Pulp Fiction* in which the male victims are made 'less-than-male'; they are feminized and thus dehumanized. I can no longer endorse an old liberalism that perpetuates a female silencing. But I cannot endorse censorship that prevents discovery of the real story either.

Why is all this so much more problematic than pornography? Perhaps because, unlike porn where all is explicit, at the heart of mainstream cinematic representations of male sexual violence towards women, there is this gap and silence. But this ellipsis, by its very nature, provides a space for the invisible to be made visible and the mute to be given voice.

The renowned screenwriter Jean-Claude Carrière recently protested self-censorship: 'Every artist has an obligation to murder his father and rape his mother.' Aside from Carrière's androcentricity (how does a woman rape her mother?), on the whole I agree with him. His words remind me we have to analyse the most ancient stories of western tradition to discover how female and male sexuality has been constructed around naturalized representations of rape that posit women as innately vulnerable and dumb.

I chose to hold on to my ambivalence because although cinematic representations of rape provide a trope that denies the embodied female experience, they also reveal an elision which makes it possible to discover that which has previously been hidden. From this perspective we can launch protest and change.

Horror: On the Edge of Taste

Mark Kermode

The difficulty with The Evil Dead *is that the name of the game is excess in the first place. To cut something that's meant to be over the top, so that it's no longer too far over the top, is very difficult.*

British chief censor James Ferman, May 1990

Like its literary antecedents, horror cinema has always focused in upon the fluctuating boundaries of taboo. It is, by its very nature, a genre of film-making which relies upon transgression. It demands that the audience's sensibilities be affronted, that decency be damned (albeit temporarily), that rules be broken. Although sadly little mainstream horror cinema challenges its audience to reassess the nature of taboo (Stephen King argues that visions of monstrousness simply make us feel more comfortable with the norm), even the most narratively reactionary, moralistic horror movies feed upon the ecstatic shock of speaking the unspeakable, of showing the unwatchable.

To the censor, horror cinema presents an insurmountable problem; how to make acceptable a brand of film-making which, at its very best, strives to be thoroughly unacceptable? Their answer, to the eternal detriment of the genre, has been clumsily to neutralize and anaesthetize cutting-edge horror movies, blunting their very point and (more often than not) stripping them of whatever radical power they once possessed. For those few movies whose power remains undiminished by the piecemeal hatcheting of key scenes, outright bans are enforced as a last resort. Ironically, to the censor, the more inventive and effective a hard-core horror movie, the more likely it is to be butchered and banned. Only anodyne or unchallenging mainstream fodder can expect to be whisked through the censors' hands intact.

To highlight this problem, let us turn our attention toward the British Board of Film Classification (BBFC), a body that exemplifies

Vol. 24, no. 6, 1995

the fundamental inability of censors to deal with horror cinema. A small and relatively conservative island, Britain has for many years been sheltered from the more excessive traits of European and American cinema by the BBFC, which classified and cut (or rejected outright) films submitted for public exhibition. Like the Motion Picture Association of America (MPAA), the BBFC has no legal standing in the cinema, but is purely an internal self-regulating 'advisory' body. Nevertheless, local councils with whom the power to permit or ban the exhibition of films resides, respect and enforce the BBFC's decisions, with few exceptions. As a result, films without BBFC certificates are effectively banned from exhibition in Britain.

Despite former chief censor John Trevelyan's 1973 declaration that cutting movies intended for adults was pointless, the BBFC have diligently hacked away at any material that could be considered contentious for years. When dealing with horrow films, their penchant for cutting the visual pay-offs from which horror derives much of its visceral power and pleasure is extraordinary. Only in Britain could a horror fan be asked to tolerate the tedium of Lucio Fulci's *Zombie Flesh Eaters* without the reward of the movie's single moment of startling shock: the on-screen piercing of an eyeball, which stares in disbelief at an approaching wooden stiletto. The effect, to which British horror fans have long become accustomed, is not unlike listening to a comedian's routine from which the punch-lines have been studiously removed. One can only imagine how funny the act was intended to be.

More disturbingly, a number of taboo-breaking horror classics whose artistic integrity has proved unbreachable by the censor's scissors have simply been banned outright in the UK. In the mid-1970s Tobe Hooper's *The Texas Chainsaw Massacre* and Wes Craven's *Last House on The Left* (both of which are now widely regarded as milestones in the development of horror cinema) were banned in their entirety after cuts failed to diminish their power. 'It's a very difficult film to cut,' said BBFC chief censor James Ferman of *The Texas Chainsaw Massacre*, which was submitted to the Board three times in various states of dismemberment, only to be airily dismissed each time. 'There's so little actual on-screen violence. However, there's lots of mental torture. It's almost impossible to change the nature of the film.' In other words the movie (which acclaimed director John Carpenter has correctly described as 'riding brilliantly along the very edge of taste') was simply too well-constructed to be rendered impotent by cuts. The result – an outright ban.

*

In the 1980s, the British censors' campaign against challenging horror movies was given an ironic boost by the rise of video. In its infancy, the video industry provided the UK with the only audio-visual entertainment which was not subject to some form of institutionalized regulation, other than notoriously vague obscenity laws. Spotting a loophole in the cinema censors' tight net, a few industrious entrepreneurs on both sides of the Atlantic took the opportunity to release on video movies that had previously been denied general theatrical exhibition. In the USA (and indeed much of Europe) this new medium would prove a saving grace for horror movies: despite the often stringent regulations of the MPAA, which still forces directors to cut or tone down their work for mainstream cinema release, distributors remain free to release unrated, uncut movies on videotape. Although certain chains like Blockbuster Video refuse to deal in such material, a relatively wide specialist audience can be reached through independent video outlets, mail order, and even record and book stores. Hence, unrated videotapes of horror classics such as *Blood Feast, Last House on The Left* or *The Texas Chainsaw Massacre* are generally available in the USA, as are uncut versions of such mainstream fare as Tony Scott's *True Romance* and Paul Verhoeven's *Basic Instinct*.

In Britain, however, the situation is quite the reverse. After an early anarchic heyday in which such international horror classics as *Driller Killer, Cannibal Holocaust* and *I Spit on Your Grave* became briefly available on UK video, tabloid newspapers mounted a campaign against the new 'threat', which they labelled 'video nasties'. In a wave of media-promoted hysteria, which would be bizarrely repeated 10 years later, horror videos were promptly blamed for everything from inattentiveness at school to muggings and rape, with headmasters, clergymen and politicians calling for drastic measures to protect the country from video dealers, who were labelled 'merchants of menace'.

Ironically, most video dealers were as eager as anybody for some form of regulation to be implemented since it was them, rather than video distributors, who were open to prosecution under the Obscene Publications Act (OPA) if their wares were judged objectionable. There were, at that time, no official guidelines as to which videos were unacceptable, and even films that had been passed for cinema release were not safe from prosecution under the OPA. Although some video versions of films contained scenes that had been cut for theatres (as with Tony Maylam's *The Burning*), other titles such as Lucio Fulci's *House By The Cemetery* and Sam Raimi's *The Evil Dead* were considered impoundable on video in exactly the same format as the

157

BBFC-approved cinema prints. Advising a newsagent whom he had recently acquitted of video obscenity changes, a judge in Wales offered the following advice: 'Remember, if it's dubious, it's *dirty!*' Meanwhile, the director of public prosecutions drew up a list of around 60 actionable titles, which included such bland fare as *The Beyond, Inferno, Terror Eyes, Funhouse, Madhouse, Evilspeak,* and *Visiting Hours.* Ironically, this list, affectionately known to horror fans as 'The Big 60', soon became an indispensable check-list of collectable titles for enthusiasts throughout the country.

Finally in 1984, following a landslide Conservative election victory, the government passed the Video Recordings Act (VRA) under which the BBFC were empowered to classify and cut all video releases with 'special regard to the likelihood of video works ... being viewed in the home'. Under these terms, it was tacitly agreed that videos should be judged more harshly than films because they could be rewound, reviewed and thus re-edited at will, and because videos classified for adult viewing only *could* be accessed by children. In 1994, the censorious terms of the VRA were extended by a Criminal Justice Act amendment that instructed the BBFC to be more aware both of the distress caused to young viewers who may view horror videos, and the supposed harm which youths who had viewed such videos may be inspired to wreak upon society. For the BBFC, these legal developments have provided a virtual *carte blanche* for further assaults upon horror cinema in all its forms.

Take the case of *The Evil Dead,* director Sam Raimi's gruesomely satirical first feature, which rapidly became a *cause célèbre* both of horror film and video censorship. First submitted to the BBFC in 1983, this violent, slapstick horror-comedy, which specifically strives to elicit a reaction of shocked hilarity from its audience, was granted a theatrical 18 certificate with 40 seconds of cuts, enforced to reduce its 'gross-out' potential. In February 1983, Palace Video released this cut version onto the rental market, unfortunately coinciding with the rise of press-fuelled hysteria over 'video nasties'. When *The Evil Dead* was finally submitted for a VRA certificate late in 1985, the BBFC banned the title outright. According to BBFC deputy director Margaret Ford: '*The Evil Dead* has been found obscene in several courts, ... [thus] it is incumbent upon us not to pass it, because obviously we would be in breach of our duties to do so.'

Five years later, in 1990, Ferman finally approved a new version of the video, after having cut an additional 65 seconds from seven separate scenes. Rather than cutting any scene in its entirety, the BBFC attempted instead to moderate the video's excessive tone, most notably in their trimming of the notorious 'tree rape' sequence, which remains, but loses its final shot of a branch shooting between the victim's legs. Other cuts detailed in the censors' report include: bloody clawing at man's face; zombie's wrist being cut; blood spurting from stump of arm; chopping of a body with an axe (all the former being from one scene); zombie's clawing of a wound in a man's leg which is already bleeding; reduction of man charging into zombie with a wooden post (from the graveside scene). The movie's penultimate climax has also been trimmed, reducing the on-screen disintegration of the demonically possessed youths. This 'significantly different version' arrived on the shelves of British video dealers on 21 May 1990, where it crucially remained open to potential prosecution under the OPA. No such prosecution followed.

What is particularly significant about the BBFC's treatment of *The Evil Dead* is that (despite their proud insistence that they toiled day and night to produce a legal version of a banned horror movie) it pin-points their inability to respond intelligently (or even consistently) to material whose very purpose is to shock. As Ferman himself has candidly admitted: 'I personally don't think that this film is depraving and corrupting' – the British legal definition of obscenity. So why the cuts? According to Ferman, he is simply powerless to challenge the verdicts reached by kangeroo courts across the country over a decade ago, verdicts that were themselves clearly affected by the moral panic sweeping Britain in the early 1980s. Nor are the BBFC willing to take a stand against the tabloid press who first fuelled such hysteria, and whose blacklisting of certain titles they clearly know to be unsound. 'The tabloid press are still a symptom of *something*,' Ferman told *Time Out* magazine in 1989. 'They have their fingers on a pulse that people who read *Time Out* and the *Guardian* don't like to acknowledge.'

In 1993, the BBFC sponsored a Policy Studies Institute survey comparing the viewing habits of young offenders with those of random non-offenders. It found no evidence to support allegations of the corruption by video of minors. 'There is not much difference' in what the two groups are watching, reported Tim Newburn of the PSI. 'With reference to horror movies, or movies with a sexual content, or slasher movies ... far from being a predominance, there is relatively little evidence that those kids [offenders] are spending much of their time watching them – certainly no more than children of that age generally do.'

But have the findings of the PSI encouraged the BBFC to behave any more leniently toward the horror movies which they now know to be harmless, but which by their very nature contain material which will outrage 'the moral majority'? Not in the slightest. For Ferman, it appears, the BBFC's job is not to assess intelligently whether a horror film or video could deprave or corrupt its likely audience. Rather, it is to mutilate and dilute such material to the point that it would no longer appear outrageous to the tabloid hacks, to make aesthetically palatable that which was designed to offend. Their role is not to protect us from horror movies, but to protect themselves from bad press. For the horror fan, this is business as usual.

Director Sam Raimi reacted with weary resignation to the BBFC's massacring of his acclaimed debut feature. 'The real problem is not *The Evil Dead*,' he sighs, 'the problem is that once the people allow the censors to determine what's right and wrong for them, once they've given them that power, who's to say that a *politically* disturbing film, a picture that differs from the view of the censors *politically*, shouldn't be censored? The people of Britain shouldn't allow them that power, because they'll soon find out that other rights are being taken from them one by one, until they have no right to speak out at all.'

China: Censors, Scapegoats and Bargaining Chips

Tony Rayns

Even in the centrally planned days when the Chinese government maintained and paid for a state film industry and expected it to produce hard or soft propaganda, film censorship was a mystery. Decades of Maoist 'purges' had taught Communist bureaucrats never to stick their necks out by taking a defined position – the only exception to this rule being when the bureaucrat was making a calculated bid for greater power – and so processes like censorship were kept deliberately vague and unattributable.

Film censorship was notionally the responsibility of the Film Bureau (then under the aegis of the Ministry of Culture, now under the new Ministry of Radio, Film and Television) but it was never unusual for Film Bureau judgements to be revised or reversed, apparently on orders from higher up. Pinpointing the exact location of a 'blockage' was as impossible as getting a member of the Film Bureau staff to admit to a specific objection to a film. The only person ever held accountable for anything was, of course, the film-maker, who could be blamed for making 'mistakes', paraded as a scapegoat or even forced to retire from the industry.

Ironically, the chaos in China's film industry in 1995 is largely of the Film Bureau's own making. Ever since Deng Xiaoping's 'economic reforms' of 1984, the Film Bureau has been searching for ways to reform the film industry. The overall policy has been to move the industry from the state sector to the private sector, partly to make it more efficient and more responsive to the needs of the audience and partly to eliminate the vast state subsidies that had been propping up the studios. As in all other areas of Chinese public life, though, the shift to a market economy has been compromised at every turn by the government's absolute refusal to relax political controls and by the fact that nothing in the Party's 40-odd years of rule has prepared any film industry personnel for the role of competent management.

Of the 16 feature-film-producing studios in China, only two continue to enjoy direct subsidies from the government: the August 1st Film Studio, owned and run by the People's Liberation Army, and the Children's Film Studio, both in Beijing. The authorities also pay bills for the Central Newsreel and Documentary Studio (which has never been expected to turn a profit), but reputedly at a much lower level than 10 years ago. All other film studios are now expected to stand on their own feet economically. First they had their subsidies withdrawn. Then they were told to stop expecting unlimited credit at the Bank of China. And then they were told to start distributing their own productions in China, and to take responsibility for selling them abroad. At the same time, in response to pressure from Jack Valenti of the US Motion Picture Producers Association (MPPA), the authorities cautiously began opening the China market to American distributors. The vanguard title in Chinese release this year, appropriately enough, was James Cameron's *True Lies*.

Beijing Film Studio and Shanghai Film Studio – the country's largest – responded to these changes in three ways. First, by abandoning all their own plans for production and devolving production to a number of quasi-autonomous 'private' companies within the studio. (Most of these 'private' companies are headed by well-known directors – Xie Jin in Shanghai, Tian Zhuangzhuang in Beijing – whose names are expected to attract outside investment.) Second, by going into joint-venture productions with the new, genuinely private, film companies springing up in China's cities, most of them offshoots of real-estate and investment finance companies. And third, by turning their studios into service centres for relatively well-funded productions from Hong Kong, Taiwan and elsewhere.

The other studios, ranging from medium-sized operations like those in Changchun and Xi'an to the tiny regional outposts in places like Nanning, Changsha and Chengdu, didn't have most of those options. Massively overstaffed, carrying exorbitant overheads and incompetently managed, they are floundering along trying to stave off bankruptcy. Xi'an Film Studio, which still has loose ties with bankable directors like Huang Jianxin, Zhou Xiaowne and He Ping, thanks to its glory days under Wu Tianming in the 1980s, has managed to attach itself to a number of privately financed movies and looks likely to survive. But most of the others will have disappeared before the end of the decade. Amid this chaos, the processes of censorship have become more elusive than ever. As if to compensate for its diminished role in the film industry, the Film Bureau routinely demands minor changes in the finished films it vets for release at home and abroad, even when the film differs in no visible way from its pre-approved script. The cutting of foreign films brought into China legally for theatrical or video release has become increasingly capricious and unpredictable. New and byzantine regulations have been brought in to control the films shot in China by overseas Chinese directors, especially those from Hong Kong; but where Clara Law (who now divides her time between Hong Kong and Melbourne) has been 'blacklisted' for smuggling erotic material past the censors for her feature *Temptation of a Monk*, other Hong Kong directors (no names, no pack-drill) have done exactly the same thing with complete impunity.

No case better illustrates the Film Bureau's current mix of mercenary pragmatism and political control than its treatment of Zhang Yimou. Zhang has always been especially vulnerable to official disapproval because (unlike his contemporaries Chen Kaige and Tian Zhuang-zhuang) he comes from what the Communist party defines as a 'bad class background'; he has lived with the risk of arbitrary punishment of victimization all his life. At the same time, his spectacular international success with films like *Ju Dou* (1991) and *Raise the Red Lantern* (1992) marked him out as a prime target for official recuperation. Zhang began working for overseas producers (who offered him better pay, higher technical standards and some measure of protection from the vagaries of the Film Bureau) in 1990, right after the Tiananmen Square massacre, and 1994's *To Live* was his fourth feature in succession to be owned by a company outside China.

Clearly recognizing that the only way to save China's film industry from terminal decline was to get internationally successful directors like Zhang back working for it, the Film Bureau made *To Live* a scapegoat film. No specific cuts or changes were demanded, but the Film Bureau made plain that it had strong objections to the film. (It has not to this day authorized its release in China.) Zhang Yimou was sufficiently intimidated by this to cancel his intended visit to 1994's Cannes Film Festival, where the film was premiered by its Hong Kong producer. And when his next project, *Shanghai Triad*, scheduled to be made for French producers, was cancelled on the eve of production, it proved relatively easy to further intimidate Zhang into agreeing to make a revised version of the film for Shanghai Film Studio instead.

Since the French had already pre-sold *Shanghai Triad* to distributors around the world, the Chinese authorities allowed them to retain the international sales rights. But the Film Bureau had succeeded in bringing Zhang himself back under control. In the future, he must make films for China's studios, which will own them and hence make profits from them. The Film Bureau, meanwhile, will retain full censorship control of the films. No Zhang Yimou film in the immediate future will be allowed out of China on any terms without specific Film Bureau approval. Given these circumstances, it is of course not surprising that Zhang made *Shanghai Triad* as such a politically safe and crowd-pleasing movie.

Phase Two of the authorities' plan to recuperate 'problem' film-makers has been their approval of Tian Zhuangzhuang's quasi-private production company within Beijing Film Studio. The Film Bureau was livid when it failed to prevent the completion and international release of Tian's *The Blue Kite*, a film financed from Hong Kong and Japan which remains banned in China because Tian made radical departures from the approved script. Then, when Tian resigned from his 'work unit' to become self-employed, the Film Bureau retaliated by blacklisting him: no studio, company or individual was permitted to finance or work with him. The 'work unit' in question, Beijing Film Studio, was given its best chance yet of surviving and prospering when Han Sanping was appointed its new head in the spring of 1995. A man of the same age as the 'Fifth Generation' film-makers, Han made it his first priority to get Tian de-blacklisted. Tian was at first deeply suspicious of Han's efforts on his behalf, but eventually agreed to rejoin the studio as a producer and was given Film Bureau clearance to do so. Tian's new position is much less compromised than Zhang Imou's, but he too is now back with China's domestic film industry.

As a producer, Tian Zhuangzhuang's policy has been to give career breaks to new directors, especially those who have graduated from the Beijing Film Academy (China's only real film school), but been unable to get a job with any of the studios. The most striking development in the Chinese cinema of the last five years has been the appearance of unauthorized independent films and videotapes by these same directors. Their films and tapes, made without official permission or control, are the first to emerge from China since the Communists took power in 1949. Tian's attempts to produce new films by these directors represents not a back-door way of bringing them under state control (although everybody accepts that it will have that side-effect) but a way of retrieving them from the poverty of means which is endemic among independent film-makers the world over.

The first of the independent features was *Mama* (1990), conceived and set up by Wang Xiaoshuai but eventually produced and directed by Zhang Yuan when the Film Bureau insisted that Wang take up a junior post in Fujian Film Studio. The film was privately financed on the back of the UN Year of the Child; it centres on a woman separated from her husband who tries to hold down her job as a librarian while also looking after her retarded teenage son without help from the authorities. Zhang Yuan (a graduate from the cinematography department of the Beijing Film Academy) intersperses the story with documentary material – glimpses of real retarded children in care, interviews with their parents and other carers – and grounds the fictional material in a realistic sense of grass-roots' lives in Beijing of a kind never seen in mainland Chinese cinema before. On completion, the film was sold to the Xi'an Film Studio, which put its logo on the front, but the Film Bureau nonetheless banned it from distribution in China. A copy was smuggled to Hong Kong, from where the film began circulating internationally. The Film Bureau finally cleared *Mama* for release in China in 1993, but remains angry that the film was sent abroad without its approval.

Mama, however, inaugurated a small torrent of independently made films and tapes. By 1993, Wang Xiaoshuai had quit his post in Fujian and made his debut feature, *The Days*, on privately raised capital of approximately US$7,000. He Jianjun (also known as He Yi), who had worked as a continuity assistant on films by Chen Kaige and Zhang Imou and made a few experimental short films, had similarly rustled up some US$10,000 to make his debut feature, *Red Beads*. Zhang Yuan had gone on from *Mama* to make a series of music videos for China's rock pioneer Cui Jian; these led directly into his second feature, *Beijing Bastards*, starring Cui Jian and dealing with the confused and directionless kids who use Cui's music as the soundtrack to their lives. At the same time, video-documentary director Wu Wenguang was shooting tapes about the lives of self-employed artists in Beijing while ex-TV directors Wen Pulin and Duan Jinchuan were shooting engaged and highly respectful tapes about the Buddhist philosophies and traditions of Tibet. Also circulating underground were anonymous tapes about Beijing's students in the aftermath of the Tiananmen Square massacre.

All these films and tapes have one thing in common beyond the fact that they were made 'illegally' in the eyes of the Film Bureau: they all spring from their makers' desires to deal with aspects of their own lives and experiences that they found either missing from or misrepresented by the state's official art and broadcast media. *The Days* offers a piercingly truthful account of the psychological and emotional problems besetting China's impoverished urban intellectuals in the 1990s; *Red Beads* constructs a tragi-comic metaphor for young people's struggles to stay sane while rejecting the tenets of traditional (Confucian) morality. The fiction films also share a remarkably frank and matter-of-fact attitude to questions of sexual behaviour and identity; this alone would be enough to guarantee banning by the Film Bureau if the films had been financed and produced within the system.

The Film Bureau's first direct action against the independents was to bring pressure on the financier of Zhang Yuan's third feature, *Chicken Feathers on the Ground*. The man was sufficiently frightened to halt the production less than a week after it started; it eventually resumed as an approved project with a different director. (The abrupt curtailment of the original shoot and the consequent discussions were documented by Zhang Yuan's wife Ning Dai in her tape *A Film is Stopped*.) Then in March 1994, after Zhang Yuan, Ning Dai and Wang Xiaoshuai had attended the Rotterdam Film Festival with their work, the Film Bureau issued its notorious blacklist, proscribing six named individuals and one video collective from producing further 'illegal' films and tapes.

Encouragingly, the only visible effect of the blacklist has been to spur the independent film-makers to greater creative heights. Zhang Yuan's riposte to the Film Bureau was to make *The Square*, an observational documentary about Tiananmen Square – not only the most public space in the whole of China but also the country's symbolic heart. Zhang is now completing a docu-drama called *Sons*, dealing with the real-life relationship between a mentally unstable alcoholic and his two drop-out sons, and plans to go on to make a feature about Beijing's gay subculture. He Jianjun completed his second feature *Postman*, poised as acutely as *Red Beads* between black comedy and tragedy, dealing with the elusive status of privacy in Chinese society. Wang Xiaoshuai has also shot a second feature, as yet unedited, and the cinematographer Wu Di directed *Goldfish*, a comedy drama about the desire (widespread among young people in China's cities) to emigrate. And underground video production continues to proliferate.

It says a lot about the lawlessness prevailing in China today that the Film Bureau's blacklist was unable to put a stop to independent film and video-making. In the China of the mid-1990s, it is always possible to find an official who will turn a blind eye to some infraction of the rules in return for a modest kickback, or a company that will provide a service for a 'blacklisted' client if the client has ready cash to spend. More intriguing is the Film Bureau's evident reluctance to act directly against the independent film-makers by, for example, rescinding their passports or taking them to court for flouting censorship and export regulations. The wild card in play seems to be the fact that the independent films and tapes have been exported and warmly received around the world. This apparently deters the Film Bureau from jumping on the film-makers as other sections of the Chinese government have jumped on human rights activists, labour activists, dissident writers and others. The international visibility of the films and tapes directly protects the people who made them. The more people who see films like *Beijing Bastards* and *Postman*, the more valuable the films become as bargaining chips in the struggle for a genuine freedom of expression in China.

A Matter of Perception

Roman Polanski

Interview by Judith Vidal-Hall

'There is no absolute evil, no single truth; everything's relative.' Ever since seeing *Rashomon* many years ago, the multiple vision – 'there are more than two sides to every story' – has been an important element in Roman Polanski's work. As has the naturalism that results from studied precision and perfection with the camera. 'I fought for realism from the beginning. I wanted to make death dirty, like it is; involve people in the guilt. Not the clean, tidy death in 1960s US movies. Death is squalid: no grand gestures.' He cites the 'real' violence confronting us daily: the terrible, unheroic images from former-Yugoslavia and Rwanda today; Vietnam and Cambodia earlier. And, like many, sees the real villain in TV, the great 'mixer', that makes entertainment out of real-life drama and confuses the outcome of both. 'Look at the O. J. Simpson soap': and mimics the swirling theme tune and 'designer graphics' that introduce each episode.

Mood, atmosphere is important: claustrophobia, fear, tightly contained within the rigours of the classic unities. It's the menace, the imminent threat of disaster, and the sudden, unexpected 'always just a little before you expect it' shock of violence, more than excess of the real thing that have earned the reputation.

Violence is 'the world we live in' and evil's no more than 'what you think is evil'. A startling assertion from someone who saw the rest of his family disappear into Nazi concentration camps, his mother for ever, when he was around eight years old and who himself survived the Krakow ghetto only by disappearing into the hostile and precarious security of a primitive Catholic Polish countryside. Other events in the life seem no less absolute: like the bizarre and brutal murder of wife and unborn child by the Manson gang in Los Angeles in 1969.

But he persists. We don't talk about World War II Poland, but neither apartheid nor torture and disappearances in Latin America change the dictum. 'Depends where you're standing, the angle of vision. Apartheid wasn't evil to the guys who were winning . . .'

This multi-faceted vision, the refusal to subscribe to clear-cut categories – victim-victimizer, good/evil, light/dark, guilt/innocence – the membrane separating victim and tormentor is porous – has much to do with the success of the latest film, *Death and the Maiden*, a tight, claustrophobic thriller in which suspense and the shadow of a doubt are sustained to the last shot. Even beyond. The end remains as ambiguous as the opening shots. As the film develops against the background of a violent storm, a power failure puts out the light and cuts off communication with the outside world. In semi-darkness, the camera cuts between the three protagonists, becoming, in turn, the champion of each: the tortured wife, the eminent human rights lawyer commissioned to examine events under the dictatorship – but not all of them – and the good Samaritan doctor whom the wife believes to be her tormentor. Each has a version of events, an angle on the truth.

Based on the play by Chilean writer Ariel Dorfman, *Death and the Maiden* is a tale of crime, punishment and forgiveness; retribution and reconciliation. Reconciliation/retribution, suggest the film-maker, are two sides of the same coin. There is no forgiveness: we go on living, tormentor and victim, in daily proximity.

Even in Communist Poland, where his first feature, *Knife in the Water*, ran foul of the censors for avoiding a politically correct resolution, Polanski has steered clear of any obvious political engagement. So why the Dorfman, an obviously *engagé* piece of work? 'Apart from the fact that I loved its enclosed, claustrophobic character, it's about human rights, guilt and responsibility in society. How you deal with the past. Even if you agree that Paulina [the wife] is right and that Miranda [the doctor] is guilty, you still have a problem. Do you deal with those people in the same way they dealt with you? It's all over the world: the old Communist countries for instance. Poland has had so many changes, censorship made a travesty of our history since the beginning of World War II: so many histories untold; so many blank spaces.'

Polanski, too, has a lot of past to deal with. Forgive? 'Never. Forget. That's the only way people can go on living together in a society.' And he has made it quite clear in the autobiography, *Roman by Polanski*, that that is how he personally handles the horrors. At a deep, uncombed subterranean level they may inform his films; the latter are not autobiography.

More than any other film-maker, Polanski has been dogged by the confusion of life and art. Critics, to his justifiable irritation, constantly cross-dress the personal life and public work. And, as always, the pundits want it both ways: after the brutal murder of his second wife, Sharon Tate, by the Manson group, it was a case of 'if a man makes films like that' – when the then recently released *Rosemary's Baby* in mind –'then of course he courts such macabre happenings.' On the other hand, 'with an experience like that behind him and the childhood, no wonder he makes the films he does'. The conviction and imprisonment for statutory rape in 1977 completed the circle and compounded the myth to the satisfaction of outsiders.

No need to talk about the life; here's the man. 'I know what I am, what I've done and haven't done.' Eighteen years' exile in Paris have rooted the hobgoblin in something solid: marriage and a child. He bounces in on sprung sneakers, jeans and a monogrammed tee-shirt, clearly bored at the prospect of another interview. Polanski is about as accomplished an actor as he is director. A pose is easily assumed, until a new direction engages a questing mind, still, with child-like curiosity, searching for answers to some of the harder questions.

As the man who more or less reinvented the genre that hovers on the murky border between violence and horror with *Repulsion* (1968), Polanski has been pursued by a reputation for gratuitous violence, a favourite target of the victims or moral panic and censors who watch the fine detail in expectation. Even *Chinatown*, considered his masterpiece and one of the finest pieces of film-making in modern cinema, has been thus tagged. It is a complex, densely plotted thriller with a Chandler/Hammett look-alike private eye played by Jack Nicholson, and set in 1930s LA. Its subject matter is corruption and incest; the political and personal violence that characterizes both. Polanski jump cuts from clock-watching boredom to extreme animation. This is something he knows about; really knows. He savages the myth of power as much as the absurdity of the censorship it drags in its wake, and cries foul at the would-be censors of *Chinatown*.

'Something very subtle goes on in front of the camera, it's about feelings, emotion: something happening in the eye – camera, actor, audience. Those tyrants, Nazi, Communist, knew that.' Reflectively. Then bursts out, 'We're talking here as though cinema were an abstract power; something separate from life, acting on its own. I just don't believe that. Nothing has the power of reality.' And he relates how, after watching *Schindler's List*, he got in a whole lot of post-World War II documentary footage on the camps and ghettos of the Third Reich for the benefit of his much younger French wife who knew little of the history. 'I had a sister, Annette. She died not long ago. One day, soon after seeing all this stuff, Emmanuelle, my wife, said to her, "That's funny, I sometimes write telephone numbers on my arm like you." She had no idea what she was seeing. Even after all those films, it just wasn't real until that moment. That's power – reality.

'And you can't have it both ways,' he insists. If cinema doesn't have that sort of power, then the arguments of the censors – corruptor of children, copy-cat crimes, the instigator of violence and horror – won't work either. 'Fuck the censors. They're preposterous; an imposition on society. Who the hell do they think they are telling me what I can read or see? Who are these people who are allowed to watch all this? What do you do with them at the end? Lock them up in an insane asylum? Put them in prison because they've become a danger to society or to themselves? Or should we give them compensation for exposing themselves to images, like we do to people who get exposed to radiation?'

But above all it's 'absurd'. Censorship ends up locking people into darkened rooms. Another anecdote. In his biography, Polanski describes how the boy Romek was, from very young, passionate about cinema. Most of the time that meant surmounting barriers of one kind or another to watch the forbidden fruit. Often simply to overcome the lack of money. Under the Nazis, for the escapee from the Krakow ghetto, that meant the Aryan joys of Leni Riefenstahl – 'Oh, they were so beautiful those films' – in the early Communism, the odd delight from Hollywood or the best in Soviet propaganda. 'One day, when we finally got as far as the door to the auditorium, we found it locked! My God, they had locked the audience in so they couldn't leave until they'd seen the whole thing!' Positive propaganda; positive uncensorship. 'What the Polish censors didn't like about *Knife in the Water* was the lack of a positive message. Send the wrongdoers to prison, or make them confess the whole thing at the nearest police station, they suggested.' Attempts to protect the European film industry by imposing quotas on US films would also, he laughed, now in fine humour, 'end up by locking French audiences into French films'.

It's a lot of effort to get up and go out to the cinema, he says, and if you get yourself together to do just that, a little plaintively, people should leave alone. When it comes to video 'that I bring back into the privacy of my home, it's no different from censoring books in the public library.'

'Television', he concedes, looking at the handsome set in a room of the large Avenue Montaigne flat that serves as office and home, 'could be a little bit different. It's only a piece of furniture but it talks to you, confronts you with images without warning.' And yes, as a recent father of a two-and-a-half-year-old daughter, Morgane, he's thought about the great excuse, the 'it's all to protect the children' argument. Of course the sensibilities of children must be protected from the most violent images. 'But because my daughter doesn't like storms doesn't mean we shouldn't ever film storms. Children are to a great degree self-regulating in what they watch, and more resilient than we think in dealing with their fears.'

As for adults, in France, 'we have explicit sex in all possible combinations on TV, and nobody's harmed.' Adding, and not for the first time, 'It's only in Britain you have this problem.' It's not the only time he refers to the peculiarity of Anglo-Saxon attitudes. Maybe confession is the answer, proffers the Jew to the English? As for the USA, 'it's all about rating certificates, distribution, who'll take the film and what's the marketing going to be like; there's no censorship as such.'

As to *Chinatown*, critics including the head of Paramount at the time, who howl about too much blood, 'don't know what they've seen'. Like Newton on optics, or Einstein on relativity, Polanski has a general theory on violence in the movies. 'There are three elements that amplify our perception of violence: we've identified with the character (who is killed in the last frame of the film), invested a lot of emotion in her, it's a shock when she dies. Then, the entire film was very realistically made, it looks, you know, truthful, the details, the acting, the use of the camera. There's not much blood but what there is is authentic. And, you know, it's not so much what you see as what you imagine you see.' And he quotes from Richard Gregory's *Eye and Brain*, as he did years ago in the autobiography, and now, precisely, from memory: 'Gregory says our perceptions are shaped by the sum of our visual experiences. We see far less than we think we see because of past impressions stored in our mind. When people came out from *Rosemary's Baby*, they were convinced they'd seen the baby, cloven hooves and all. All they'd really seen, for a split second, was a subliminal superimposition of the catlike eyes ... We perceive much less than we imagine we do.' But wait a minute; can the millions be that wrong? He insists: it's the baggage we carry around. 'Violence is the world we live in.'

Not that anything much is left to the imagination by the new boys like Tarantino or even veterans like Oliver Stone. 'It's all terribly explicit now but it's less effective. I fought for reality and look where it's got to. A little blood goes a long way. I hate all this blood splashing around the screen. It looks phoney, unreal, almost a spoof. Because we haven't invested anything in these characters, the only shock is in the violence, not an assault on the emotions.' But he concedes that the world changes and it's a lot to do with style. 'The language of cinema has changed. There's a new grammar, more pace.' Like literature. 'We wouldn't, after all,' he asks, 'expect a novel of the late twentieth century to read like Zola or Dickens, would we now?'

Jack Nicholson said of him, 'That little Polish bastard is one goddam genius,' adding, 'whatever anyone says about his private life, I know he's never hurt a living soul.' The bright-eyed, half-starved on pickled gherkins, greedy for life and grasping at every sensory experience kid from the ghetto has also been called 'the finest movie director in the modern era'. That was John Huston. Nothing if not controversial, the man whom others – and he quotes – have called 'that evil little dwarf', slowly comes into focus in the no-man's land where victim and victimiser meet. Suddenly you know who he is: little Oscar, the boy with the tin drum who refused to grow until the grown-ups put their world to rights. Brilliant fantasies and 'too much reality'.

He denies reports that he's about to make a World War II movie in Poland, or even has plans to go back there. 'The haemorrhage of talent from Poland was worse than anywhere. The decay is physical as well as mental.' The 'great expectations' he observed on his visit there in 1981 have subsided; he wasn't at all sure that the situation in the film industry was easily reversible. He spoke about his 'beloved' Mikhail Bulgakov (*Index* 8/1991), the uncompromising Russian master of the surreal, and author of *The Master and Margarita*.

Rich in irony, ambiguity and with flights of fantasy unsurpassed in twentieth-century literature, now there's a challenge for a man whose first film, *Two Men and a Wardrobe*, was, they say, a miniature masterpiece of the surreal. So much for realism.

Festivals, Films and Fireworks

Nadezhda Pokornaya

Just before my September trip to Moscow I came across a photograph of MosFilm studios in *Le Monde* and it frightened me. The once renowned studios resembled the city of Stalingrad after the last bombing attack of World War II. Yet what I saw when I got there was nothing of the kind. MosFilm had been transformed from a film studio into a complex consisting of 10 independent studios. Of course instead of producing 150 films a year as they did in the wasteful days of hard-core socialism, MosFilm today makes at most 30, a figure, like everything else these days, dictated by the free market: none of the former republics of the USSR, now independent states, can any longer be forced to purchase Russian films.

Like the city of Moscow itself, MosFilm looks something between a heap of debris and a construction site – but only at a first glance. Those who visit Moscow regularly can see that practically everything is in a ferment of reorganization; its hardly surprising that at this stage nobody can guess what the prospects are for any future enterprise.

A couple of months ago the multi-million dollar XIX Film Festival resounded throughout Moscow. The money was allocated by prime minister Viktor Chernomyrdin from the state budget – money that should have been used on new films. Fireworks danced in the Moscow sky in honour of the festival while Russian film-makers looked on and counted: there goes my pre-production, and there's the stock and the cutting equipment ... Guests from the West were lavishly welcomed with caviar and champagne, taken on boat cruises. Their entertainment programme was exceptional, even including a prison 'reception': the chairman of the festival, Richard Gere, spent one night in Nizhny Novgorod remand centre for purchasing 25 kilos of poachers' caviar. Subsequently his agent apologized for this incident from the stage, assuring the audience that Mr Gere was not a speculator. Everybody applauded hysterically as a token of sympathy. The critics who related this to me couldn't conceal their sarcasm; they are gloomy about the situation in the film industry. 'There used to be slogans all around us saying "THE ARTS BELONG TO THE PEOPLE!" Now it's clear without any slogans that our diseased arts belong to the diseased people ...'

Russian cinemas are overloaded with western thrillers and erotic films. Russian films are not being advertised or purchased by distributors for mass demonstration. A recent sociological poll suggests that the culture of cinema-going can never be revived. To boost profits, managers of uncomfortable and untidy cinemas are compelled to rent their space out for discos and as sale rooms for western cars. There is a lot to be said about the problems of distribution, but there is little doubt that for those who control it, the 'blockade' of Russian films on the home market is a profitable business. On the other hand, take Vladimir Menshov's film *Shyrli-Myrli*. Financed by MosFilm and RosKomKino, it cost US$7 million, enough for the average budget of six films. The film was particularly well advertised and distributed and became more popular than all the American thrillers.

The state continues to sponsor its favourite directors. Thus *To love à la Russe* [director Eugeny Matueev] was made exclusively on the funds provided by the Ministry of Finance. Meanwhile at the XIX Film Festival the Russian minister of cinematography made an appeal to the Russian people to contribute money for the sequel to this blockbuster. 'Make the first "people's" film!' On which my friend Olga Henkina, a critic, commented: 'I pity those who have not yet seen *To love à Russe*. It's now my favourite film. I used to think the summits of idiocy were conquered, but I was wrong. Marvellous film! There's never been better quality pornography. If the director films a bare bottom, then he does it in such a way that nobody would want to look at any other. How skilfully the protagonist tries to get under his female co-star's skirt. After seeing that you'd never want sex again ...'

In the course of my visit – just eight days – I watched the rapid politicization of film-makers who appeared on television and radio. Many eminent directors and actors have hastily joined the ranks of various parties and political blocs on the eve of the elections, as if in response to a war-cry: 'The place of an artiste is in the State Council!' Politicians have always exploited artistes; some may really believe culture will save the world, others simply get what they can out of the famous names.

In the last two years the subject-matter of films has changed. The age of pornography and dark, heavy films is coming to an end and the latest fashion is Russian melodrama. According to Paola Volkova, a tutor at the Higher Screenwriters/Directors School, 'The pendulum of art is swinging in the other direction. It had become too much of a formula and the reaction has now set in.'

Volkova is right. For five years we have been learning all sorts of filth about ourselves; this filth was transferred to the screen and, frequently, vice versa. The Frankenstein monster stepped from free, post-Soviet Russian cinema into life. At first it frightened everybody a good deal, then it started to get on people's nerves like an obtrusive fly. Now people are starting to forget about it. Violent feature films have lost their appeal for film-makers as well as their audiences. Only Frankenstein's half-dressed bride still appears now and then in newly fashionable erotic melodramas. But for some reason she covers her face, as, for example, in Svetlana Illyinskaya's *The Masked Sinner*, co-written with US and German screenwriters. The film is about a very beautiful actress disfigured in a car crash. Since she cannot afford plastic surgery, she takes a job in a sex show, hiding her face under a veil. Her objective is not only to earn some dosh, but to prove the power of her talent and recover her face, evidently by revealing her backside. Advertising insists this 'gripping' film is potentially a winner with distributors.

To be fair I should say that there are other films and their number is increasing. Many directors have turned to classics: Roman Balayan – Turgenev's *First Love*. Vladimir Dostal – Solugub's *Small Devil*. A Sakharov – Pushkin's *A Young Peasant Lady*; and several directors are indebted to Chekhov. Under dictatorship escapist cinema was made to avoid the nausea of social realism. Nowadays, directors are tired of quasi-democracy. Besides, there's no need to beg money from sponsors when they can get state funds for Pushkin.

In the course of the last two years, films on the new Russians, by the new Russians, and frequently financed by the new, right-wing bourgeoisie, have begun to appear on the Russian market. They are about people – or to be more precise, about certain types – who encapsulate the essence of our time. For example, Denis Evstigneev's *Limita* and Valery Todorovsky's 1995 *Moscow Suburban Nights*. They have divided the critics, so I went and asked Todorovsky about the effect of the abolition of state censorship on films and about the problems directors were having to cope with now.

At first we saw freedom as a blessing. But now this freedom has turned into problems – a fear of freedom has emerged, problems of choosing subject, genre, money, of film financing. Directors have divided into two groups: those capable of surviving competition and those who were crushed by it. The viewers have their freedom – now they choose what they want to see. Distributors deal only with what is profitable. All this threatened the Russian film industry with disintegration. But it has recovered. A new entity has appeared on the Russian market – producers. They brought the rules of survival in the free market. There are victims, but some have gained – me, for example. I have accepted the need to find financing for new films, on top of being just a creator; it's part of the job, not a tragedy. Abolition of state censorship has brought freedom of travel and we started going to western countries, to the festivals; wherever I went I made new friends in the film industry. But the free market is traumatic. Many one-time successful directors had to step aside – such stars of the 1970s cinema as Eldar Ryzanov, Vitaly Melnikov, Igor Maslennikov, Semyon Aranovich. On the other hand, Mikhalkov continues working and very successfully. The Oscar for his *Burnt by the Sun* is a victory after all. The current situation is especially hard on the generation whom so far nobody knows. A beginner has to make a talented half-penny film so that he is noticed and considered worth financing. To survive, a director has to make one film a year. A cameraman costs up to US$20,000, rent of equipment US$5–6,000. *Love*, which I made in 1992, cost 900,000 roubles, while *Moscow Suburban Nights* in 1994 cost US$5,000,000 and was financed by the French Film Aid Institute. I consider myself very lucky professionally. I have managed to survive in this new financial war.

In an interview with the monthly *Kino-glaz* (Cinema Eye) this year, director Sergei Solovyev, chairman of the Union of Film-makers of Russia, spoke about this new world.

With the disintegration of the USSR the social system, which guaranteed work to everyone who had a degree, has disintegrated as well. In the last couple of years production of films has substantially reduced, the threat of unemployment has reared its head, professional criteria were lost – those who managed to find the money would make the films. At present we have surmounted the crisis of the industry, largely owing to the fact that the Union of Film-makers, has been preserved. Today Russia produces about 100 feature films per year, 90 of them financed by the state (with funds provided by sponsors). Out of those 100, two to three are very good, 10 decent. While in the past popular production was based on the taste of Party bosses, now it caters for the most common, vulgar taste of an average viewer. We don't have censorship as we did in the past and it's unclear what's worse; the ugliness in our films exceeds anything on the world screen. The tastes of those with the money become the criteria for evaluating a film. Our cinematography has never been the financial phenomenon it is in Hollywood; it has always been guided by cultural values. Andrei Tarkovsky said film is the highest form of poetry. The empire is a thing of the past and politically we are deeply divided now. Cinema guided by true art should unite us.

It's Good out in the Jungle

Milos Forman

Interview by Sally Sampson and Judith Vidal-Hall

'Everything that is noble, and that has remained in art and literature since ancient times and that is also significant for strong contemporary works of art, has always concerned itself with injuries and injustices against the individual. That is because we always perceive the work of art as individuals. There, at the bottom of all those great works of art, are the injustices which no social order will eliminate.'

High sounding sentiments, pompous even, from a man who professes to have no time for the moral abstraction or heroic ideal. Neither in life nor in art. Maybe it's just a case of the word made redundant: failing to achieve what the image has already done so many times and so much more succinctly.

In the flesh, as in his films, Milos Forman presents a different image. Urbane, quiet, a European of the enlightenment despite almost 30 years in the USA; huge energy contained behind thick, heavily-framed lenses, somehow larger than life in the genteel pastiche rococo of one of Paris's more discreet hotels favoured by those of a publicity-hungry business who seek privacy rather than the paparazzi.

He engages with ideas, coiling back on an earlier thought to develop an idea in perpetual motion, talking the while of such things as the perils of freedom or dictatorship, the survival of small nations, the 'absurdity' of censorship, the over-rated power and passing pleasure of the movies, the ambivalent joys of the Internet – just another means of distribution – and the rights of individuals, life, art and what passes for both, not as one who panders to these particular concerns out of courtesy, but with passion informed by experience. His next film, *The People Versus Larry Flint* (1996), confronts free expression head on. Almost; it's more an out-flanking approach.

'Larry Flint was the editor of *Hustler*, the lowest form of bad taste pornography. But we own him a lot. The magazine was sued by the right-wing moral crusader Jerry Falwell in the 1980s and Flint ultimately censored by a bullet that paralysed him and left him in constant pain. He became a junkie, his wife took an overdose. He had his spinal cord severed; there was no pain, but no control over his bodily functions either. He went cold turkey, made a million dollars and took his case to the supreme court. He got the most important judgments ever for free expression in America.'

There's the paradox again: noble victories in a lousy cause. Not so lousy: 'The first thing the Nazis and Communists attacked were sex, deviation, pornography. Prostitution's older than censorship, you'll never beat it, but it was an excuse to inflict fear and impose power; everything else followed. Today it's the right-wing militias who're screaming loudest for a free press. Freedom *is* indivisible, even when it brings to power those who will curtail it for others. Excesses are the price we pay to protect it for all. I remember the films of Leni Reifenstahl. They were beautiful. I loved them. I don't think they touched my feelings, but they probably left an impression at the time. If anti-Nazi stuff had also been allowed, rival propagandas could have fought it out.'

Born in small-town Czechoslovakia in 1932, Forman has been a participant, willing or not, in most of the 'big ideas of our time': Nazism carried off both parents to die in concentration camps when he was a child; Communism dominated and then curtailed his working years in Czechoslovakia; Hollywood beckoned and he was plunged into the delights and despairs of market capitalism. Having sampled all, the realist has time for none. There is a paradox – a favourite word that peppers his conversation and provides a unifying motive in works as different as *One Flew Over the Cuckoo's Nest*, *Amadeus* or *The Firemen's Ball* – at the heart of freedom as in the mind of the dictator. Human nature is ambiguous; the individual will always be at odds with any system; outsiders that society can neither comprehend nor contain will be the victims of even the most benign social order. Forman films have no larger than life heroes or anti-heroes as do US films and fables: the genius Mozart is neither the appealing child prodigy nor the uniform high-tone man; the fixed grimace of the criminally insane – perhaps? – McMurphy who turns the well-meaning establishment on its head, is no conventional liberator of men. His approach to the ambiguities and complexities of man and systems is that of a pessimistic humanist: 'The individual will never win these battles; the people in the system have a right to their lives too.' But an optimist in the long-term evolution of systems and the survival of the spirit that opposes their instinct to control. His tools are a compassionate humour, tragi-comic irony that looks beneath the surface and finds things not quite as conventional wisdom would have us believe. Genius is rejected by mediocrity – all systems are mediocre – but the high priest of the mediocre, Salieri, blesses his tribe as he passes through the ranks of his fellow lunatics, misfits and rejects in his old age at the end of *Amadeus*. The teenagers of the 1960s who reject and are rejected by an older generation in *Taking Off*, are no more lost or confused than their middle-American parents. It's circumstance that makes people what they are, not moral absolutes or fixed notions of right and wrong, good and bad. 'Milos Forman works with the ordinary, everyday reality of things,' says Jack Nicholson, morally ambiguous star of *One Flew Over the Cuckoo's Nest*.

It's as true of the glossy big budget productions of post-1968 as of the gentle, ironic humour of the comedies made in Czechoslovakia before Prague's New Wave cinema was rudely cut off by Russian tanks.

1968 found Forman in France, where *The Firemen's Ball* was representing Czechoslovakia. Despite its success with audiences who recognized themselves and their situation and welcomed the comic relief, trouble with a government that saw only an anti-government indictment of corruption and incompetence at the highest level ruled out return. A timely invitation to Hollywood snatched him from the path of the advancing tanks; back home, *The Firemen's Ball* was privately dubbed, 'The last laugh in the face of the Russians'.

He was a reluctant exile: 'I was never a dissident, only a bit subversive. You do what you want or have to and other people stick on the labels.' And in odd counterpoint to the friend who stayed on, Jiří Menzel, adds, 'In any case I never thought it would be so long. Just a couple of films to prove I could make it out there. Who would have thought 22 years....' For the whole of which all his films, along with most of the irreverent New Wave, were banned, including, *Amadeus*, the first and only film made in Prague since he left. 'They didn't want us, but we made them a financial offer – lots of hard currency – they couldn't refuse. Even so they treated us as though we didn't exist. The media were forbidden to mention us, the film wasn't shown until 1990. But everyone saw us filming in the streets; everybody was talking about it. That's the absurdity of censorship: people know what they are told they do not know.'

But Prague, after all, is the city of Kafka as well as Mozart. And as Forman himself says, Communism didn't invent the genre. Given his personal insights, had he never thought of filming Kafka? 'Frequently. It's not easy, but I think about it often.'

And might he return, permanently, to Prague? No. The decision was made a long time ago, in 1975 when he took US citizenship. While he talks with fond memories of old classmates like Vaclav Havel, or brilliant teachers like Milan Kundera, nostalgia is not enough. 'It's paralysing thinking all the time one day I'll go back. You don't do anything else.'

From nightmare to dream: Hollywood, America. What were the obvious differences? Weren't the constraints of the studio system and the tyranny of the market effectively more subtle variants on the old censorship? Not a bit of it. While working in Hollywood is not without its perils, its heady anxieties are a million miles from the old certainties of Communism.

'In Eastern Europe it was like being kept in a zoo: you were in a cage but there was a roof over your head and someone fed you every day. In the USA, it's the jungle: you're free to go where you like, but everyone's out there trying to kill you. In Communist countries there's a recipe, a formula for everything. There are no signs hung out in Hollywood. You make what people want to see and what market forces determine they want.' And while the much-maligned market has its own laws, they're a good deal easier to negotiate than political ideologies. Financing what the money men consider 'uncommercial' can be a problem, not a prohibition. Nor is it something that's suddenly loomed into the forefront as one might think from the griping in Europe and other parts of the world. 'Even back in 1975, a film like *One Flew Over the Cuckoo's Nest*, not on the face of it a commercial winner – an asylum for the mentally ill and misfits turned over by a guy who is supposedly criminally insane – eventually found a backer. It was made on a budget that looks derisory today, US$1.4 million because everyone involved did it for peanuts. Even so it came out at US$4 million. Then of course, it took off and everyone was happy.' Marketing, he says with the confidence of a 10-percenter, is for the mediocre; the 10 per cent that matter will make it anyway. 'There's not one, monolithic "Hollywood",' he reflects, 'more like one behind every door; find the right door.'

He blows away French fears that US cinema with its saturation marketing and global reach will wipe out the European industry, with the thought that competition not quotas – just another form of censorship – might provoke some quality films with specific national character and appeal rather than straining to join the Americans in the game they play best.

But doesn't he fear his America is under attack from the radical, new right? Government-hating militias, religious fundamentalists, disenchanted blacks, angry white males and extremists of all kinds? 'For years I've had huge faith in America. It's self-correcting system: the pendulum swings way over to one side, an then rights itself. Look at McCarthy. It seemed as though it was the end of Hollywood. But no. I still have faith that the pendulum will right itself. America is condemned to freedom. The USA has more races, religions, languages than Yugoslavia. Why isn't there a permanent civil war? Freedom is the opposite of human stupidity. The day America forgets that it's in trouble.'

Forman has shown a prescient sense of timing with many of his films. *One Flew Over the Cuckoo's Nest* for instance. As well as picking up on the subversive, and at the time revolutionary, theories of R. D. Laing and others who reversed conventional thinking on sanity and society, it was a poignant commentary on the abuse of psychiatry in the Communist world where psychiatric hospitals became prisons for the mentally dissident.

But no: *The People Versus Larry Flint* is not a response to the growth of the radical right in the USA. The script was in the offing 'long before Gingrich and Dole got going on the big speeches'. But the tale of the sleazy purveyor of porn, outside the pale of 'decent' society winning a victory for the benefit of all Americans, could touch a chord. It's due to open around the time of the presidential elections; the stakes are higher than they've been for a long time.

Like many who were victims of film as propaganda and who as film-makers found themselves expected to produce the film with the right message rather than a personal meaning, Forman debunks 'the power of the movie', benign or otherwise. 'For a couple of hours I can be very powerful. Then audiences go out, life takes over. Film can have an effect, but something in life could achieve exactly the same effect. We most of us live vicariously. It's pure entertainment. There are only two things in life: living it and talking about it. All the rest is survival. People go to the movies to escape, to be entertained. The majority go to a movie to stave off boredom; there's only about 10 per cent who go for any real reason like seeing the work of a particular director or because they want to know what this film says.'

He talked about the flood of anti-heroes on the US screen, the Stallones, Schwarzeneggers, Willises, and found the cosy reassurance of *Forrest Gump* an interesting phenomenon. 'It's sentimental, well made and a health reaction: here's the common man and he's a hero. Americans are afraid; they don't know how to protect themselves from what they see around them and mirrored on the screen. Life and art become blurred. Look what the networks did with O. J. Simpson. The perfect drama: did he, didn't he; will they, won't they find him guilty. The lawyers are the heroes of the courtroom drama. The only solution people see is yet more guns: one in your pocket, one in mine. And calls to get tough on law and order.'

Aided and abetted by the image-makers of fact and fiction, society moves steadily to the right. And Hollywood is not much interested in eternal truths, only the eternal dream, all the better for being American. 'Telling the truth without being boring is difficult and people don't want to hear it anyway; lies are easier, more intriguing.' The secret of success for this film-maker lies in 'finding a truth that everyone knows and telling it in a way they haven't heard before.'

It's a line that holds for *The People Versus Larry Flint*. Every schoolchild knows by heart the rights and liberties promised under the Constitution; Americans everywhere still sing the praises of 'the land of the free'. It is under threat from politicians who offer to trade 'a little liberty for a little security' to a population frightened into forgetting what's at stake. And from extremists of all shades who, in the interests of one propaganda silence others, often, though not always, with the best intentions.

Maybe it needs an outsider who has lived most of his life without them and come to care for them so passionately to retell the USA what it knows so well: there is no liberty without free expression. Not by putting high sounding phrases into the mouth of an ancient constitutional grandee or right-on liberal campaigner, but through the modern history of *Hustler*.

Images of Africa

Haile Gerima

Interview by Sally Sampson

I don't have the material power to create a budget, but at least I can negotiate from my position within the Afro-American community in the USA. It is a sad thing to be born in a Third World country with so much to say and so few resources.

Few countries in Africa have a national policy on cinema: the more cinema is repressed, the better for those in power. As they say in South America, motion pictures are like a 'new hydrogen bomb': drop American movies by satellite on to a village, and that village will explode, culturally speaking. The cultural domination from outside is so strong that there is no chance of manufacturing local images.

In the francophone parts of Africa, film-makers follow a European notion of what African cinema is like; that is a kind of censorship. Instead of making a personal film about my grandmother, I'd ask myself, 'What do the French like? Something exotic!' There should be a national film policy to help African film-makers build up an archive of national memory.

Film-makers are trying to make their own personal films on video in Ghana; they will use any instrument to ingrain their humanity. This is happening in Mozambique and Ethiopia; it can be very powerful, especially if film-makers begin to realize their capacity to affect society, even if some of these videos are an imitation of *Dallas*, with some witchcraft thrown in for good measure.

In America, slavery is a very sensitive topic. The moment I wanted to make *Sankofa* (1993) my credentials in the USA vanished, because I was venturing into forbidden territory. The resource centres were closed to me: I couldn't get funding. Censorship became a reality; the funding agencies for cultural development shut their doors. They'd talk about timing: 'This year's budget is nearly spent. You're too late – or too early.' Nobody comes out with it straight and says that the subject matter is wrong. The press is much the same; they wouldn't touch *Sankofa* at Berlin, though it was in competition with big budget movies. They censor you by making you non-existent. We went to Montreal and Toronto: they skipped us, didn't even talk to us. They thought we were finished.

The film opened in Washington DC in a second-run theatre. None of the big distributors would touch it (one of them said it was 'too black'!) so we invited 20 activists from the community to see it. They opened a theatre, and the rest is history. The film was a smash hit with black people all over the country. In New York we were at the Cineplex, and got our money back. Now we're preparing a major launch on video, by mail order: we're demonstrating the marketability of the movie. Over 50,000 people in each city have signed to buy it.

Many African-American and Chicanos can't make the movies they want to make, because they don't live up to the expectations of white producers. That's why you see so many black independent film-makers playing in with Hollywood and making bizarre 'shoot 'em up and kill' movies. Black people respect Spike Lee, especially for his shrewd ability to function in that mega world; he brings many black talents into his productions. Our people see Spike walking the commercial tightrope to make something serious, and more dignified. He's at a critical stage now, and we are waiting to see what happens next.

Churches and schools came in busloads to see *Sankofa*; they are culturally hungry for a different king of movie. Most black movies make black people look very bizarre, hopelessly bizarre; this is unacceptable. Commercial film-makers sometimes leave the community unfulfilled and demoralized, asking itself: 'Is this all that blacks are capable of?' Church people complain that the romanticism and glamour associated with violence in mainstream black films trickle back into the community. While Hollywood continues to select and produce films that reflect its own view of what the black community is, this contradiction will continue.

Sankofa may well be a milestone linking African cinema to African-American cinema. It is the first time two African countries, Ghana and Burkina Faso, have collaborated on a film about slavery. But to talk of African cinema is sometimes very hard: even Ousmane Sembene, the father of African social cinema, has to wait 10 to 15 years between films, and I know 20 film-makers in Ethiopia who have not made a film in five years. They think the world is against them, but they still want to effect change.

South Africa is crucial to the rest of Africa: it has the technology and the infrastructure. But this could be a two-edged sword: it will be a platform for the USA and the rest of the West. If it merely exploits this by pumping Hollywood movies and videotapes in a very sophisticated way all the way up from the Cape to North Africa, that could be frightening. But if South Africans develop their own cinema and create an easy working platform for film-makers all over Africa, in countries where there are no laboratories, this will be to the advantage of all of us. South Africa is a crossroads.

Beyond 2001

Arthur C. Clarke

It has always seemed to me that the limits of censorship are defined by two famous quotations: Voltaire's 'I disagree with everything you say – but will fight to the death for your right to say it' and Chief Justice Holme's: 'Freedom of speech does not include the liberty to shout FIRE! in a crowded theatre.' In real life, one must attempt to steer a course between these two extremes. Thus I can tolerate astrologers purveying their (usually) harmless nonsense, but not anti-Semites and neo-Nazis hawking their poison. Even here, though, there is a fringe area: should Leni Riefenstahl's brilliant documentaries be banned because of their sponsor? And aren't there some rather embarrassing bits in *Birth of a Nation*?

As it happens, I have helped to destroy one form of censorship. Quoting from the speech I made at the UN on World Telecommunications Day, 17 May 1983, I pointed out that the development of communications satellites accessible by cheap and portable equipment would mean that 'news gatherers would no longer be at the mercy of censors or inefficient (sometimes non-existent) postal and telegraph services. It means the end of the closed societies and will lead ultimately – to repeat a phrase I heard Arnold Toynbee use 40 years ago – to the unification of the world.'

> What I am saying is that the debate about the free flow of information which has been going on for so many years will soon be settled – by engineers, not politicians. (Just as physicists, not generals, have now determined the nature of war.)
>
> Consider what this means. No government will be able to conceal, at least for very long, evidence of crimes or atrocities – even from its own people. The very existence of the myriads of new information channels, operating in real time and across all frontiers,

will be a powerful influence for civilised behaviour. If you are arranging a massacre, it will be useless to shoot the cameraman who has so inconveniently appeared on the scene. His pictures will already be safe in the studio 5,000 kilometres away; and his final image may hang you.

Many governments will not be at all happy about this, but in the long run everyone will benefit. Exposures of scandals or political abuses – especially by visiting TV teams who go home and make rude documentaries – can be painful but also very valuable. Many a ruler might still be in power today, or even alive, had he known what was really happening in his own country. A wise statesman once said, 'A free press can give you hell; but it can save your skin.' That is even more true of TV reporting – which, thanks to satellites, will soon be instantaneous and ubiquitous.

That was written more than 12 years ago: the satellite TV news gives hourly proof that this state of affairs has now arrived. Living as I do in Asia, I can also observe the impact of western movies and TV serials upon societies with totally different cultural backgrounds.

Sometimes it is hard not to sympathize with latter-day Canutes attempting to hold back the waves pouring down from the sky; what has been aptly called 'electronic imperialism' will sweep away much that is good, as well as much that is bad. Yet it will only accelerate changes that were in any case inevitable and, on the credit side, the new media will preserve for future generations the customs, performing arts and ceremonies of our time in a way that was never possible in any earlier age.

Recently I had the enjoyable task of using satellite links to address both Rupert Murdoch and Ted Turner (though not simultaneously!). I gave them this advice on the use and misuse of satellite TV. After quoting a British prime minister's famous accusation that the press enjoyed 'the privilege of the harlot – power without responsibility', I added:

Today, the TV screen is more powerful than newsprint, and whatever the bean-counters may say, responsibility should always be the bottom line.

Though I'm opposed in principle to any form of censorship, my stomach is often turned by the hideous violence shown on so many TV programmes. It's no excuse to say that Hollywood* is an even

---

* And though Hollywood may be the worst offender, it is by no means the only one. I am reminded that *A Clockwork Orange* was made in England; the only time I ever saw it was when Stanley Kubrick arranged a screening for me at the studio. Although I understand that he has now withdrawn it from exhibition, later highly praised movies have been far more violent, with far less justification.

worse offender, and I know all the arguments about screen violence providing catharsis, and not role models. But you can't have it both ways: if the advertisers really believed that, they'd never buy any air time.

I don't believe that a civilisation can advance technologically without corresponding moral progress; if they get out of step, it will self-destruct, as ours is in danger of doing.

Which leads me to an awesome conclusion. We've had TV for 50 years. Therefore a volume of space containing several hundred suns has now been filled with news of our wars, atrocities and crimes – real ones and fictional ones, which an alien intelligence might have great difficulty in distinguishing.

I conclude from this that there's no, repeat no, superior civilisation in our immediate vicinity. For if there was – the cops would already be here, sirens screaming right across the radio spectrum.

To sum up: as this century draws to a close, it looks as if all the old arguments about censorship will be made obsolete by wide-band, person-to-person communications. When you can download anything and everything 'in the privacy of your own home', as certain notorious advertisements used to say, not even entire armies of Thought Police will be able to do anything about it.

The real challenge now facing us through the Internet and the World Wide Web is not quality but sheer quantity. How will we find anything – and not merely our favourite porn – in the overwhelming cyberbabble of billions of humans and trillions of computers, all chattering simultaneously?

I don't know the answer: and I have a horrible feeling that there may not be one.